BRAZIL
PLAYER BY PLAYER

BRAZIL
PLAYER BY PLAYER

First published in the UK in 2013

© Demand Media Limited 2014

www.demand-media.co.uk

Printed and bound in Europe

ISBN 978-1-909768-64-2

CONTENTS

Introduction

Many of the finest Brazilian players started off barefoot in the favelas or on the beaches with a tiny ball made from paper or rubbish. This gave them superb close control and allowed them to practise and then develop difficult skills. Despite their obvious ability, however, the national side's early appearances didn't hint at the greatness to come. The Brazilian football federation was partly to blame as constant arguments over professionalism led to weakened sides being fielded. The first recorded match consisted of players from Rio de Janeiro and São Paulo taking on English club side Exeter City in Fluminese's stadium in 1914. Goals from Oswaldo Gomes and Osman gave the hosts their first victory. Sixteen years later, Jules Rimet, enamoured with the success of the amateur Olympic tournament, pressed FIFA to organise a professional event. Uruguay was chosen to host the first tournament in 1930 to coincide with the centenary of its independence.

The Brazilian people were immediately captivated by the World Cup, and the side was expected to do well at the first tournament. However, it was local rivals Argentina and the hosts who would make it to the final, with Uruguay winning the Jules Rimet Trophy. Four years later the football world descended on Italy and the hosts would win again. In 1938 the tournament was staged in France but Brazil were now a major force on the world stage and striker Leônidas was one of the stars of the event. He scored four goals against Poland in a thrilling 6–5 win, although Wilimowski also netted four times for their opponents. Brazil lost to Italy in the semi-final but then beat Sweden in the playoff to claim third place. The Second World War robbed many players of their best years but by 1950, with the tournament on home soil for the first time, the Brazilian public expected much from their side. They didn't disappoint, initially at least, with centre forward Ademir encompassing all that was good about South American football.

England entered the World Cup for the first time believing that as champions of the old world and indeed the old style they would have no problem bringing the trophy home. But the flair and skill of the Brazilians took the game to a different

level. They thrashed Olympic champions Sweden 7-1 in the new Maracanã Stadium in front of nearly 200,000 people and then smashed six past Spain to claim their place in the de facto final (the latter stages of this tournament were played in a round-robin format and Brazil only needed a draw against neighbours Uruguay to win their first World Cup).

The game seemed to be going to plan when Friaça put Brazil ahead, but Schiaffino equalised for Uruguay midway through the second half. Eleven minutes from time, Ghiggia broke through the Brazilian defence and beat Barbosa at the near post. Brazil had somehow snatched defeat from the jaws of victory, and the country went into mourning.

In 1954 the magnificent Magyars of Ferenc Puskas were hotly tipped to lift the Jules Rimet Trophy in Switzerland. Brazil came up against this formidable team in Bern in one of the most violent matches ever played. Hungary won

Above: *The Brazilian team for the 1930 World Cup in Uruguay*

but three players were sent off and the fighting continued amongst the players in the tunnel afterwards as well as the fans and stewards on the pitch.

Two years later Brazil came to England for the first time to play a friendly at Wembley. They were 2-0 down to the hosts within four minutes, but Paulinho rifled in a low shot from a tight angle just after the break and then Didi equalised. Tommy Taylor put England back in front with a close-range header, and

then Gilmar saved two penalties. Stanley Matthews provided a cross for Granger to head home late on and give England a 4-2 victory. It was obvious to most people watching, however, that Brazilian skill and pace would soon outdo English muscle and determination.

By 1958 Brazil had toughened up physically without sacrificing any of the flair and a 17-year-old Pelé scored a deflected goal in the World Cup quarter-final against Wales to set up a meeting with France in the semi. Vavá opened the scoring but the incomparable Just Fontaine equalised before Didi restored a slender lead for the South Americans. Pelé then stole the show with a tap in, a close-range shot with the outside of his right foot, and finally a powerful right-foot shot into the bottom corner to make it 5-2. They won the final by the same score although they went behind to a brilliant solo goal from Liedholm. Vavá equalised from a few yards and then scored an identical goal to put Brazil 2-1 up. Pelé scored a magical goal after 55 minutes by

Above: *Brazil line up for the 1959 Copa América*

semi they overcame the hosts to set up a meeting with Czechoslovakia. The Czechs took the lead through Masopust but Brazil equalised through Pelé's replacement Amarildo, and he then provided the cross for Zito to give Brazil the lead. Vavá pounced on a mistake from the Czech goalkeeper to seal the victory and back-to-back World Cups.

In 1964 Alf Ramsay's England toured Brazil to mark the 50th anniversary of their football association. Brazil took the lead but Jimmy Greaves equalised in the second half. Pelé then set Ronaldo up for his second before scoring his first and Brazil's third. He turned provider again shortly afterwards as Brazil scored their fourth. They added a fifth in the last minute and looked certain to lift the Jules Rimet Trophy for the third time in England in 1966.

Pelé scored a blistering free-kick in their opening match against Bulgaria at Goodison Park but he was constantly fouled and had clearly become the tournament's marked man. Garrincha added a second with another superb free-kick. In their next match against Hungary Pelé's knee injury kept him on the sidelines and Hungary opened the scoring, but Tostão equalised with a

flicking the ball over the defender's head and finishing into the bottom corner. Zagallo then poked the ball home to make it 4–1 but Sweden pulled one back through Simonsson. Pelé scored again with a header in the last minute, however. It was Brazil's first World Cup victory and the planet rocked to the samba beat.

Pelé scored a magnificent solo goal in Brazil's opening match at the 1962 World Cup in Chile but he then picked up an injury. Brazil avenged their Wembley defeat by knocking England out of the tournament in the quarter-final. In the fierce left-foot shot. It was a classic game with plenty of chances and Farkas then smashed home a beautiful volley before the Hungarians scored a penalty. The 3-1 defeat meant Brazil had to beat Portugal to progress and, although he was still carrying an injury, Pelé had to be recalled. The Portuguese ruthlessly cut him down, however, and Pelé's tournament ended with him being carried off the field (he did return but he was heavily strapped and made little impact). Eusébio then took control and Portugal knocked the holders out.

Pelé vowed not to play in another World Cup, but, having scored his 1000th goal in 1969 and with new coach and former team-mate Mário Zagallo now at the helm of the national team, he changed his mind and joined the side in Mexico in 1970. They went a goal down in their opening match against the Czechs but Rivelino equalised with a thunderbolt free-kick and Pelé then gave Brazil the lead before Jairzinho added another two. He then scored the winner against England in a match of such quality that it was dubbed 'The final that never was'. It was also memorable for Gordon Banks's wonder save from a Pelé header. Pelé smashed in a free-kick against Romania

in their last group game before Jairzinho added a second from a yard out and Pelé a third. Romania got a consolation but Peru were more easily dispatched. Brazil had to overcome a stern challenge from Uruguay in the semi-final but they then brushed Italy aside in the final (4-1), although they did concede a sloppy goal after a defensive mix-up. They then upped the tempo and dazzled the Italians with their supreme skill and flair. This was the beautiful game at its finest, the zenith of Brazilian football.

Four years later the side was still

Above: *The magnificent Maracanã hosted the de facto World Cup final in 1950, but Brazil famously lost to Uruguay*

Above: *An injured Pelé at Goodison Park during the 1966 World Cup. He was targeted by the Portuguese and repeatedly fouled*

rebuilding after the loss of Tostão, Gérson, Carlos Alberto and, of course, Pelé. Mário Zagallo was now coach but the side was a shadow of the all-conquering 1970 vintage and they only scraped through their group on goal difference. Rivelino kept them in the tournament with his free-kicks and they squeezed past East Germany, but they went out to the superb Dutch in an ill-tempered semi-final. They also lost the third-place match against Poland.

Four years later, Brazil were still struggling, none more so than in their match against Poland when they hit the post twice and then the crossbar

in a single move, although the ball was eventually turned in. They didn't lose a match in the tournament but were eliminated on goal difference when hosts Argentina controversially and somewhat suspiciously put six past Peru. They then scored two wonder goals to take third place ahead of Italy.

The side was tipped to do well in 1982 as a new golden generation of players like Zico, Sócrates, Júnior and Falcão were now in their prime. In their first match against the USSR the Soviet Union took the lead but Sócrates and Éder smashed in wonderful long-range efforts to seal the win. They also went behind against

Scotland but Zico, Oscar, Éder and Falcão scored to give Brazil a comfortable win. Zico scored a scissor kick and then a second from close range to see off New Zealand, and Brazil then overcame a tame Argentina. But they came unstuck against a Paolo Rossi-inspired Italy in a pulsating game that was eventually decided by some poor defending.

In 1984 the best goal scored in the Maracanã came from the boot of an Englishman, John Barnes. His mazy dribble past five defenders and smart finish heralded a decline in Brazilian football that wouldn't be addressed for another decade. The 1986 World Cup team showed flashes of brilliance – such as Josimar's two wonder goals – but they ran into Platini's France in a quarter-final of intoxicating brilliance. Careca opened the scoring but France equalised through Platini. Then Branco was brought down in the box and Zico stepped up to take the penalty but it was saved by Joël Bats. The keeper also saved Sócrates's spot-kick in the subsequent shootout, but Brazil were thrown a lifeline when Platini put his penalty into orbit. Júlio

Above: *Zico attempts an audacious bicycle kick at the 1982 World Cup in Spain*

César then hit the post and Fernandez won the game for France with a cool strike into the bottom corner.

Four years later Brazil were struggling to find the next generation of superstars, but the side was still in transition and could only squeeze past Sweden, Costa Rica and Scotland in the group stage. They were then knocked out by Argentina. In 1994 Brazil could finally boast some of the best players in the world and in Romário and Bebeto they had two of the most feared strikers. Goals from Romário and Raí helped them overcome Russia and then they cruised past Cameroon, but they could only draw with Sweden. A late Bebeto

goal saw them edge past hosts USA in the first knockout round, and more goals from Romário, Bebeto and Branco were enough to beat the Netherlands in the quarter-final. Romário was on target once more in the semi against Sweden and Brazil finally won their fourth World Cup with victory over Italy in a penalty shootout after a poor game.

Brazil made the final four years later at France '98 after wins over Scotland and Morocco, although they suffered a surprise – but irrelevant – defeat to Norway in their last group match. They demolished Chile in the last 16 and needed goals from Bebeto and Rivaldo to edge past Denmark in the quarter-

Left: *Ronaldo collides with Fabien Barthez in the final of the 1998 World Cup in Paris*

final. They then beat the Netherlands on penalties to secure a final berth against the hosts. In the build-up to the match Brazil's star striker, Ronaldo, suffered a suspected seizure and the team was off its game in the final. Two Zidane headers and a late Petit goal gave the hosts victory but Brazil would bounce back in style four years later in Japan and South Korea. With a fit Ronaldo, Brazil won their group with three wins, saw off the challenge from Belgium, England and Turkey in the knockout stages and eventually beat Germany 2-0 in the final to claim their fifth World Cup.

Despite the loss of Bebeto, Ronaldo and Rivaldo in the build-up to the 2006 World Cup in Germany, the side easily topped its group but it wasn't strong enough to challenge for the top honours and came unstuck against the French in the quarter-final. They reached the same stage in South Africa in 2010 having again topped their group and beaten Chile in the last 16, although they were then beaten by a Dutch side that out-muscled and out-worked them.

The 2014 World Cup will be held in Brazil, and many of the players featured in this compilation of the 100 greatest footballers to represent the country will be hoping to cement their reputation in another golden era for Brazilian football by winning the trophy for the sixth time.

Ademir

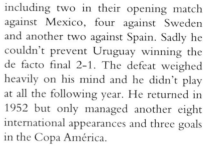

Ademir enjoyed an 18-year domestic career with Sport Recife, Fluminese and Vasco da Gama, but it was his nine years with the latter club that defined him as a player of supreme skill and one of the greatest centre forwards in the game's history. He was quick over short distances and immensely powerful, and his sublime finishing and unmatched skill elevated him above every other player in the world. In all he made 429 appearances for Vasco da Gama, scored 301 goals and secured five state championships.

He was called up to the national team in 1945 and made an impact in the Copa América (12 goals in 18 starts overall) with a tournament-winning hat-trick in 1949. In 1950 the World Cup came to Brazil and he partnered Zizinho and Jair in a deadly three-pronged attack. He scored an incredible 14 goals in nine starts during the build-up and in the tournament itself, including two in their opening match against Mexico, four against Sweden and another two against Spain. Sadly he couldn't prevent Uruguay winning the de facto final 2-1. The defeat weighed heavily on his mind and he didn't play at all the following year. He returned in 1952 but only managed another eight international appearances and three goals in the Copa América.

He retired from all football in 1957 to concentrate on commentating and coaching. How he must have enjoyed watching the team he had inspired lift the World Cup in Sweden in 1958.

Name: Ademir (Marques de Menezes)
Born: November 8th 1922, Recife
Died: May 11th 1996, Rio de Janeiro
Position: Striker
International Career: 1945 - 1953
Caps: 39
Goals: 32
Honours: Copa América (1949), World Cup Runner-up and Golden Boot (1950), Pan-American Championship (1952)

Adriano

Above: *Adriano at the Copa America*

Adriano started playing youth football with Flamengo and then graduated to the senior team for a season, during which he made 19 league appearances and scored seven goals. He then moved to Europe and joined Internazionale, although he was shipped out to Fiorentina on loan and then had two years with Parma before returning to Inter for five years. Despite scoring another 47 goals in 115 league appearances and winning four Scudettos, he was voted the worst player in Serie A three times in five years.

He was initially tipped as a long-term replacement for Ronaldo and he made his debut for Brazil in a World Cup qualifier against Colombia in 2000 aged only 18. But it took him three years to score his first goal in the yellow jersey (at the 2003 Confederations Cup). Despite leading the line and scoring another two goals, Brazil were eliminated at the group stage. He bounced back during the 2004 Copa América and won the Golden Boot with seven goals, including the 93rd minute equaliser against Argentina in the final, which Brazil eventually won on penalties. He was also the best player at the 2005 Confederations Cup, and he steered Brazil to victory over Argentina again with two goals in the final.

He was included in the 2006 World Cup squad but, despite scoring twice, he lived up to his inconsistent tag and only managed five shots during the entire tournament. His international career then declined, although he was recalled for the qualifying campaign for the 2010 World Cup. He was omitted from the final squad, however, so he saw out his domestic career with Flamengo, Roma and Corinthians. If he can find some form, he may return to the international scene in time for the 2014 World Cup on home soil.

Name: Adriano (Leite Ribeiro)
Born: February 17th 1982, Rio de Janeiro
Position: Striker
International Career: 2000 – 2010
Caps: 48
Goals: 27
Honours: Copa América (2004), Confederations Cup (2005)

Alberto

Carlos Alberto signed for Fluminese when he was 19 and he racked up nearly 100 appearances and nine goals, but it was only when he moved to Santos three years later that he became a global superstar. In eight years for the club he made 445 appearances and scored a half-century of goals, and it was on the back of these performances that he cemented his place in the national team. (He had made the 44-man training squad for the 1966 World Cup in England but he wasn't included in the final 22, which was a surprising decision given his leadership and flair.)

When João Saldanha was tasked with restoring pride to the yellow jersey, he chose Carlos Alberto as the national captain. Four years later all the pieces were in place for the side to reap the benefits at the 1970 World Cup in Mexico. Perhaps the finest team ever assembled in the modern era romped through the initial group stage with wins over Romania, defending champions England and Czechoslovakia. With Carlos Alberto at the helm, the side then dispatched Peru (4-2), Uruguay (3-1) in the semi-final, and Italy (4-1) in a one-sided final. He scored the best goal of the tournament and one of the greatest goals of all-time after the ball had been passed around the entire team. When Pelé eventually laid the ball off on the edge of the Italian area, Carlos Alberto thundered in from right back at full tilt and rifled the ball into the bottom corner of the net.

It was to be his only appearance at the World Cup, however, as a persistent knee injury ruled him out of the 1974 tournament in West Germany and seriously limited his speed down the flank when he was eventually passed fit. He was selected by coach Claudio Coutinho to captain the side for the first three qualifying matches for the 1978 World Cup but, as he hadn't played for seven years and was now 33, he'd lost his edge and retired to join several former greats like Pelé and George Best at New York Cosmos.

He moved into coaching in 1983

with Flamengo and then flitted amongst a number of clubs before ending up as the national manager of Azerbaijan in 2005. He resigned after assaulting the technical referee and suggesting the match officials had been bribed after his side lost against Poland.

Apart from this brief controversy, Carlos Alberto's career only attracts the highest praise. He captained the greatest side in the world, was listed as one of Pelé's greatest living footballers in 2004 and was then included in the World Team of the 20th Century. If his knee hadn't kept him out of the national team for seven years, he would surely rank alongside Pelé, Maradona, Messi and Cristiano Ronaldo as one of the greatest players of all time.

Name: Carlos Alberto (Torres)
Born: July 17th 1944, Rio de Janeiro
Position: Right back
International Career: 1964 – 1977
Caps: 53
Goals: 8
Honours: World Cup Winner (1970)

Aldair

Aldair began his career with Flamengo but he moved to Europe after four years and 185 league appearances to join Benfica. He only remained with the Portuguese side for a season but he then transferred to Roma for 13 years and more than 400 appearances. He first played for the national team in 1989 but it wasn't until 1994 that he achieved the success his talent deserved: a World Cup winners' medal.

Four years later Aldair was again in the centre of defence for their World Cup campaign in France. Despite progressing comfortably to the final, Brazil were outplayed by the hosts and two Zinedine Zidane headers and a late Emmanuel Petit strike sealed victory for the French. Aldair finally retired in 2010 after only playing 27 league games in the previous seven years.

Name: Aldair (Aldair Nascimento dos Santos)
Born: November 30th 1965, Ilhéus
Position: Central Defender
International Career: 1989 – 2000
Caps: 81
Goals: 3
Honours: Copa América (1989, 1995, 1997), World Cup Winner (1994), Confederations Cup (1997)

Alves

Dani Alves made his professional debut for Bahia in 2001. After 25 appearances he was loaned out to Sevilla and, having helped the national youth team to the 2003 world title, the move was made permanent. He stayed with the Spanish team for six years, during which time he collected the UEFA Cup, 175 caps and 11 goals, but he then signed for rivals Barcelona in 2008 for a reported £23 million. A number of separate financial clauses made him the world's most expensive defender but he repaid the faith and the outlay by helping the team win the 2009 Champions League (he was suspended for the final), the Copa del Rey and La Liga. The side retained the league title for the next two seasons and also won its fourth Champions League.

Alves's superb form attracted the attention of the national team and he made his debut in 2006 in an unofficial friendly against Kuwait. He then provided an assist and scored a goal to help the team win the 2007 Copa América against archrivals Argentina. He came on in the 2009 Confederations Cup semi-final against South Africa and scored the winner but, despite his extraordinary free-kick ability and hefty price tag, he has often been overlooked by the national selectors in favour of Maicon. However, he has still managed to collect 62 international caps, score five goals in the yellow jersey, and make more than 500 appearances overall.

Name: Daniel Alves (da Silva)
Born: May 6th 1983, Juazeiro
Position: Right back
International Career: 2006 –
Caps: 62
Goals: 5
Honours: Copa América (2007), Confederations Cup (2009)

Antônio

Marco Antônio began his career with amateur side Fazenda FC but he was soon picked up by Portuguesa, although he only remained with them for a single season. In 1969 he joined Fluminese as a versatile defender who played at left back but often ventured into midfield with darting runs up the flank.

He was called up by the national squad before the 1970 World Cup in Mexico but he wasn't expected to start in a team that included Brito, Carlos Alberto, Wilson Piazza and Everaldo, but he came on after an hour against Romania in the last of the group matches and started the next game against Peru, which Brazil won 4-2. He was back on the bench for the semi-final against Uruguay and again for the final against Italy, both of which were comfortable wins for the Pelé-inspired Brazilians.

He was still playing his club football at Fluminese when he joined the national team at the 1974 World Cup in Germany, but the wonder team of 1970 had disintegrated and Brazil were not the force they once were. They still made the semi-final but were beaten comfortably by the new Dutch masters. Marco Antônio was included in the squad for the qualifying campaign for the 1978 World Cup in Argentina but he didn't play in the finals themselves and retired soon afterwards.

Name: Marco Antônio (Feliciano)
Born: February 6th 1951, Santos
Position: Left back
International Career: 1970 - 1979
Caps: 52
Goals: 0
Honours: World Cup Winner (1970)

Baltazar

Baltazar began his club career with União Monte Alegre in 1943 but it wasn't until he signed for Corinthians two years later that this devastating striker made his name. He stayed with the club for 12 years and scored 267 league goals in only 401 appearances. He was called up to the national team for the 1950 World Cup on home soil and scored against Mexico in Brazil's opening game. He scored again in their match with Switzerland but couldn't prevent Uruguay winning the Jules Rimet Trophy in the second phase.

He represented his country again in 1954, and he again scored in Brazil's opening match against Mexico. He missed vital chances against Yugoslavia in their second group match and was an unused substitute in the infamous match against Hungary in Bern, which Brazil lost 4-2.

His international career over, Baltazar saw out his club days with Juventus and Jabaquara before joining União Paulista for a final season in 1959.

Above: *Baltazar*

Name: Baltazar (Oswaldo da Silva)
Born: January 14th 1926, Santos
Died: March 25th 1997, São Paulo
Position: Striker
International Career: 1950 – 1954
Caps: 31
Goals: 17
Honours: World Cup Squad (1950, 1954)

Baptista

Júlio Baptista began his professional career with São Paulo and made 75 appearances before signing for Sevilla in 2003. He was a prolific goal-scorer in his first two years in Spain, netting 50 times in only 81 appearances in all competitions. He then joined Real Madrid but came to Arsenal on loan in a swap deal with José Antonio Reyes in 2006/07. He maintained his scoring record and was soon snapped up by Roma, where he stayed for the next three seasons, before joining Málaga.

He was first picked to represent Brazil in 2001 but he couldn't cement his place in the side because he was often played out of position by his domestic clubs and his form suffered as a result. He did play under Dunga at the 2010 World Cup in South Africa but the tournament was a disappointment and Brazil were eliminated by the brutal but brilliant Dutch in the quarter-final.

Name: Júlio (César Clemente) Baptista
Born: October 1st 1981, São Paulo
Position: Attacking midfield
International Career: 2001 – 2010
Caps: 47
Goals: 5
Honours: Copa América (2004, 2007), Confederations Cup (2005, 2009)

Barbosa

Barbosa was a diminutive figure who played professional football from 1940 with ADCI-SP via Santa Cruz and Vasco da Gama to Campo Grande in 1962. He refused to wear gloves because he wanted to feel the ball in his hands after every shot, and he soon became one of the best goalkeepers in the world. He was called up to the national team in 1949 and was between the sticks for the 7-0 thrashing of Paraguay that secured that year's Copa América. He was also on duty during the 1950 World Cup on home soil.

Brazil reached the decisive match and were expected to beat neighbours Uruguay comfortably, and they duly scored first. Uruguay equalised, however, and in the 79th minute Alcides Ghiggia drilled the ball past an out-of-position Barbosa and sent a nation into shock. Barbosa was blamed for the error for the rest of his life and he was shunned by the Brazilian football establishment.

He died broken and penniless of a heart attack in 2000.

Name: Barbosa (Moacir Barbosa Nascimento)
Born: March 27th 1921, Campinas
Died: April 7th 2000, Praia Grande
Position: Goalkeeper
International Career: 1949 - 1953
Caps: 17
Goals: 0
Honours: Copa América (1949), World Cup Runner-up (1950)

Bauer

Bauer started his career with São Paulo but then signed for Botafogo, winning six state championships between 1943 and 1953. He was selected for the national team before the Copa América in 1949 and helped the side win the tournament. He played in the following year's World Cup but couldn't prevent Uruguay winning the de facto final. Four years later he was captain of the squad for the 1954 World Cup but his tournament ended after the infamous Battle of Bern in which there were 42 free-kicks, two penalties and three red cards. The fighting continued between the players and fans well after the match.

Having retired from playing, Bauer took over as manager of Ferroviária de Araraquara. While touring Mozambique with the team he spotted Eusébio and recommended that São Paulo sign the talented youngster. The Brazilian side refused so Eusébio went to Benfica instead.

Name: (José Carlos) Bauer
Born: November 21st 1925, São Paulo
Died: February 4th 2007
Position: Midfield
International Career: 1948 – 1954
Caps: 29
Goals: 0
Honours: Copa América (1949), World Cup Squad (1950, 1954)

Bebeto

B ebeto began his professional career with Vitória but it was only after moves to Flamengo and Vasco da Gama that he made an impression on South American football. He made 133 league appearances for the clubs between 1983 and 1991 and scored 62 goals. In 1992 he signed for Deportivo La Coruña and further enhanced his reputation with another 86 goals in 131 league starts over the next four years. In 1993/94 he famously refused to take a penalty that would have given the side its first La Liga title. Miroslav Đukić took it instead and missed, handing the title to Barcelona.

Bebeto made his international debut in 1985 but he missed the following year's World Cup because coach Telê Santana decided to go with a more experienced front line. He didn't make much impact at Italia '90 but with his strike partner Romário he was one of the stars at the next tournament in the USA. He scored three goals en route to the final, which Brazil won after

Roberto Baggio missed his penalty for Italy in the shootout. He will also be remembered for his goal celebration having put Brazil ahead against the Netherlands: he ran to the sideline and rocked an imaginary baby as his wife had just given birth. (His son, Mattheus, is now with Flamengo but has been offered a contract with Juventus.)

Four years later Bebeto played a supporting role to Ronaldo and

Rivaldo as Brazil once again made the final. He had started in the last 16 match against Chile and scored against Denmark in the quarter-final, and then he started against the Dutch in the semi. He probably should have taken a bigger role when Ronaldo was taken ill before the final but Ronaldo recovered and chose to play, although the whole side was a shadow of the team that had dominated the tournament and they lost to hosts France 3-0.

He retired from international football after the World Cup but continued playing at domestic level for various clubs in his homeland until 2002. He then briefly coached América.

Name: Bebeto (José Roberto Gama de Oliveira)

Born: February 16th 1964, Salvador

Position: Striker

International Career: 1985 - 1998

Caps: 75

Goals: 39

Honours: Copa América (1989), World Cup Winner (1994), Confederations Cup (1997)

Bellini

Hilderaldo Bellini was of Italian descent but he was born in Brazil and began his professional career at Vasco da Gama. He was a solid and skilful central defender who liked launching counterattacks from deep within his own half. He soon moved to São Paulo FC and ended his domestic career with Atlético Paranaense. It was on the international stage that he will be best remembered, however.

He first played for Brazil in 1957 but he was such an influential figure that he was selected as captain for the 1958 World Cup in Sweden. Brazil duly swept the other teams aside and battered France and hosts Sweden (both 5-2) in the semi-final and final respectively. It is down to Bellini that whenever a team wins a trophy the captain collects it and holds it aloft, which he pioneered in Sweden so that the press could see the Jules Rimet trophy. This gesture was immediately recognised as a symbol of triumph and it has now become the norm for all captains in any sport.

Bellini played in the team that won

Above: *Hilderaldo Bellini holds the Jules Rimet Trophy aloft in 1958*

the 1962 World Cup in Chile and he also appeared at the following tournament in England, although he only played two matches, a 2-0 victory over Bulgaria and a 3-1 loss to Hungary. He retired immediately after the defeat and Brazil were then eliminated by Portugal.

At the end of his career he was honoured with a statue outside the national football stadium, the famous Maracanã, showing him lifting the World Cup.

Name: Hilderaldo Luís Bellini
Born: June 7th 1930, São Paulo
Position: Central Defender
International Career: 1957 – 1966
Caps: 51
Goals: 0
Honours: World Cup Winner (1958, 1962)

Branco

Branco joined Internacional at the age of 16 but, after only 15 league appearances, he signed for Fluminese. He stayed with the club for five years before coming to Europe and playing for Brescia, Porto and then Genoa. He was a goal-scoring left back who inspired the likes of Roberto Carlos with his ferocious free-kicks.

He made his debut for Brazil in 1985 and started the first match of the 1986 World Cup in Mexico against Spain. His side won 1-0 and repeated the result against Algeria in their second outing. Branco was also in the side that beat Northern Ireland to make it through at the top of their group. They then thrashed Poland 4-0 and he scored his penalty against France in the shootout at the end of the quarter-final, but when Sócrates and Júlio César missed they were eliminated.

He also made the starting line-up at the 1990 World Cup and played in all three lacklustre group matches, even though Brazil won them all by a single goal. He was also in the side that was eliminated by Maradona's Argentina at the Stadio Delle Alpi in Turin. Four years later the team was much stronger both physically and mentally but Branco was only on the bench for the group-stage matches. He scored a trademark free-kick from distance to knock the Dutch out in the quarter-final, and he then started the semi-final against Sweden. He also took one of the successful penalties in the final against Italy. In all, he managed to score nine goals in 72 appearances for his country.

He retired from international football the year after the World Cup but he played on domestically with Flamengo, Corinthians, Middlesbrough, the Metro Stars and Fluminese before retiring for good after problems with his weight in 1998. He returned to the game in 2012 as manager of Figueirense.

Name: Branco (Cláudio Ibrahim Vaz Leal)
Born: April 4th 1964, Bagé
Position: Left back
International Career: 1985 - 1995
Caps: 72
Goals: 9
Honours: World Cup Winner (1994)

Brito

Brito joined Vasco da Gama aged 16 but he soon established himself as a defender of considerable skill. He was nearly 6'3" and solidly built so he was good in the air and had the strength to ease opposing forwards off the ball. His distribution was superb and he was another player who liked to launch attacks from deep. He had one year with Internacional but then returned to Vasco da Gama from 1960 until 1969.

It was during this period that he was called up to the national team and he went to the 1966 World Cup. He only started one match, however, the 3-1 defeat to Portugal that saw Brazil eliminated from the tournament. Their opponents had clearly targeted the flair players like Pelé and it was a brutal game that showcased the worst of football. Four years later, the team would reconvene in Mexico determined not to let any opposition defenders get anywhere near them.

They demolished Czechoslovakia 4-1, squeezed past England 1-0 and Romania 3-2, then beat Peru in the quarter-final 4-2, Uruguay in the semi 3-1, and Italy in the final 4-1. The team was undoubtedly at the peak of its powers and most of the flowing moves stemmed from the back, with Carlos Alberto and Brito particularly influential.

His club career wound down after spells with Flamengo, Cruzeiro, Botafogo and Corinthians but he didn't retire until 1979.

Name: Brito (Hércules de Brito Ruas)
Born: August 9th 1939, Rio de Janeiro
Position: Central Defender
International Career: 1964 - 1972
Caps: 45
Goals: 1
Honours: World Cup Winner (1970)

Cafu

Cafu was raised in the Jardim Irene favela in São Paulo, but he soon developed into a footballer of considerable ability. By the age of seven he had enrolled with a football academy but he was then rejected by the Corinthian, Santos and Portuguesa youth teams. Instead he found himself on the bench for the São Paulo juniors. Coach Telê Santana then suggested he try playing wing-back instead of midfield and Cafu immediately repaid Santana's faith by guiding the senior team to two Copa Libertadores (1992, 1993) and being named South American Footballer of the Year (1994).

He'd been called up by the national team in 1990 but he couldn't cement his place in the side and was only a substitute at the 1994 World Cup in the USA. However, an injury to Jorginho early in the final against Italy meant he got to play the next 100 minutes. The game went to penalties and Brazil lifted the trophy after Roberto Baggio's miss. Cafu was a revelation and was rarely out of the national team for the next 12 years.

He guided the team to his second World Cup final four years later in Paris against hosts France, but Brazil were off their game because star striker Ronaldo had suffered a seizure in the build-up. The qualifying campaign for the next tournament saw Cafu sent off against Paraguay and then stripped of the captaincy by Wanderley Luxemburgo. When the coach was dismissed, new manager Luiz Felipe Scolari chose Émerson as his captain but the skipper dislocated his shoulder in training and Cafu regained the armband.

He was again inspirational and led the team to his third World Cup final, a unique achievement by a player. He lifted the trophy after Brazil's 2-0 victory over Germany, but thereafter the team's fortunes declined and he was partially blamed for its poor performance at the 2006 World Cup in Germany. Coach Carlos Alberto Parreira was heavily criticised for relying on veterans like Cafu and Roberto Carlos and Brazil were

beaten 1-0 by France in the quarter-final.

Cafu initially wanted to continue until the 2010 World Cup in South Africa but by then his club career, which had been suitably glittering with Roma (Scudetto in 2001) and Milan (Scudetto in 2004 and Champions League in 2007), was in decline and he retired from football in 2008. He remains the only man to have played in three World Cup finals and his blistering pace, overlapping runs, leadership and honours for club and country ensure that he will forever be regarded as one of the great right backs and captains.

Name: Cafu (Marcos Evangelista de Moraes)
Born: June 7th 1970, São Paulo
Position: Right back
International Career: 1990 – 2006
Caps: 142
Goals: 5
Honours: World Cup Winner (1994, 2002), Copa América (1997, 1999), Confederations Cup (1997)

Caju

Caju began his senior career with Botafogo. After five years he joined Flamengo, and from there he moved to Marseille and Fluminese before returning to Botafogo. He won several state championships with the latter and was called up to the national team after the disappointment of the 1966 World Cup in England when Brazil were dumped out in the group stage. Caju was one of the playmakers who helped Brazil to World Cup glory in 1970, and he provided many assists for the likes of Pelé, Tostao, Rivelino and Jairzinho. In all he won 57 caps and scored 10 goals in his decade-long international career.

Name: (Paulo Cézar Lima) Caju
Born: June 16th 1949, Rio de Janeiro
Position: Attacking midfield
International Career: 1967 - 1977
Caps: 57
Goals: 10
Honours: World Cup Winner (1970)

Careca

Careca had six years with local side Guarani, during which he scored 38 league goals in 63 appearances, before he signed for São Paulo. After netting 54 times in 67 games he was lured to European giants Napoli where he spent an equally productive six years (73 league goals in 164 games) alongside Diego Maradona and Bruno Giordano. He helped the Italians to the UEFA Cup in 1989 and the Scudetto the following year. After Maradona left, he formed a solid striking partnership with a young Gianfranco Zola.

He was drafted into the World Cup squad for España '82 but missed the tournament after picking up an injury. Four years later he showed the world what it had been missing. He scored five goals in five matches before Brazil were knocked out by Platini's France on penalties in the quarter-final. He returned for the World Cup in Italy in 1990 but by then was past his best and he could only manage two goals before Brazil were beaten by archrivals Argentina in a disappointing second round. He last played in the yellow of Brazil in the qualifying campaign for the 1994 World Cup, although he was overlooked for the tournament itself because of the emergence of Romário and Bebeto.

With more than 250 goals, Careca remains one of the world's greatest strikers, although ill-fortune and injury denied him the greatest prize. It also didn't help that Brazil were a side in transition throughout much of his international career. He continued at club level in Japan and back in Brazil until 1999.

Above: *Careca at the 1986 World Cup in Mexico*

Name: Careca (Antônio de Oliveira Filho)
Born: October 5th 1960, Araraquara
Position: Striker
International Career: 1982 – 1993
Caps: 64
Goals: 30
Honours: World Cup Squad (1986, 1990)

Carlos

Roberto Carlos was born in Garça near São Paulo in a poor neighbourhood and he spent his time doing odd jobs on a farm and playing football with friends. His domestic career began with União São João, for whom he made 33 appearances from 1991 to 1993 and scored 10 goals. He then signed for Palmeiras and Internazionale before agreeing a big-money move to Spanish giants Real Madrid in 1996. He made the left back position his own for the next 11 years, racking up 584 starts and scoring 71 goals for a side that won four La Liga titles and appeared in three Champions League finals.

Having been voted the best left back in the world alongside Paolo Maldini, Roberto Carlos was called up for the Brazil squad in 1992, although he wasn't selected for the World Cup in the USA two years later. He helped the side to the Copa América in 1997 and then scored a remarkable free-kick against France in Le Tournoi. He struck the ball with the outside of his left foot from about 35 yards and although it initially appeared that it would fly well wide of Fabien Barthez's goal, it suddenly curled back into the bottom corner.

He played in all seven matches at France '98 but couldn't help a lacklustre Brazil still reeling from Ronaldo's shock collapse overcome the hosts in the final at the new Stade de France. He exorcised the demons four years later in the Far East and was voted into the World Cup's all-star team after Brazil had beaten Germany in the final, 2-0. He played in his third and last World Cup in Germany in 2006 but he was blamed by many fans for failing to mark Thierry Henry effectively in their 1-0 quarter-final loss to the French. Carlos reacted angrily to the criticism and announced his international retirement.

Having returned to Brazil in 2010 to play out his club days with Corinthians, Roberto Carlos hoped to feature in Dunga's squad for the upcoming World Cup in South Africa but he, along with Ronaldo and Ronaldinho, were not included in the 23-man party. In 2011 he turned his attention

to managing Anzhi Makhachkala, a side in the Russian top flight.

Roberto Carlos was a scintillating player with great skill, balance, power and pace. His ferocious shooting and longevity – during his career he amassed 820 appearances and 101 goals – mean he stands alongside Italy's Paolo Maldini as the greatest left back in the game's history.

Name: Roberto Carlos (da Silva Rocha)
Born: April 10th 1973, São Paulo
Position: Left back
International Career: 1992 – 2006
Caps: 125
Goals: 11
Honours: Copa América Winner (1997, 1999), Confederations Cup Winner (1997), World Cup Winner (2002)

Castilho

Right: *Carlos José Castilho in action*

Known as the 'lucky man' by opponents, and Saint Castilho by Fluminese fans, Castilho had a reputation for pulling off miraculous saves and having more than his fair share of good fortune. He played for club side Fluminese for 17 years (1947 - 1964) and was called up to the Brazilian World Cup squad for every tournament between 1950 and 1962, although he only made three appearances at the 1954 finals in Switzerland. Brazil were a potent force but they were knocked out by Hungary in the brutal Battle of Bern.

Four years later Brazil lifted the World Cup and they defended the title in Chile in 1962 but Castilho was no more than a peripheral player. In 696 games for Fluminese, however, he only conceded 777 goals, and he kept a record 255 clean sheets. Aside from his obvious ability, he was also known as extremely brave. He once partially amputated his finger to save having another operation on it, and he was back playing within two weeks. He retired in 1964 to concentrate on coaching but committed suicide in 1987.

Name: (Carlos José) Castilho
Born: November 27th 1927, Rio de Janeiro
Died: February 2nd 1987
Position: Goalkeeper
International Career: 1950 - 1962
Caps: 3
Goals: 0
Honours: World Cup Squad (1950, 1954, 1958, 1962)

César

Júlio César began his career with Flamengo in 1997, and he became the club's first-choice keeper the following season. His impressive domestic record led to him being called up to the national squad before the 2004 Copa América, which Brazil went on to win. By 2005 he'd racked up 130 appearances for Flamengo and was being courted by a number of top European clubs. He signed for Italian giants Internazionale and helped them to third place in Serie A behind Juventus and Milan in 2007. They were then awarded the title after the other two clubs were embroiled in a match-fixing scandal. By 2012 he'd played more than 300 times for the club and won five Scudetto league titles, the Italian Cup, Super Cup and the Champions League. He then surprised the football world by signing for Queens Park Rangers who were tipped to struggle in the English Premier League.

He was called up to the Brazilian national squad as cover for Dida in the 2003 Confederations Cup but he didn't play. He collected his first cap during the 2004 Copa América campaign and played all six matches. They made it to the final against Argentina but the game went to penalties. César blocked the first spot-kick and Brazil went on to win 4-2.

He had to take a backseat for the next three years after Dida's return and he only collected another seven caps. He missed out on the 2005 Confederations Cup and the 2007 Copa América and he was only third choice for the 2006 World Cup. Dida retired after the tournament so César was left to fight against Heurelho Gomes and Doni for the number one jersey. By 2007 he had established himself as Brazil's best keeper and he helped them to the 2009 Confederations Cup with a 3-2 victory over the United States.

César was first choice for the 2010 World Cup in South Africa but he was blamed for their defeat at the

hands of the Dutch and was dropped. However, a solid domestic start with QPR earned him a recall for the international friendly against England at Wembley in early 2013. He couldn't stop the hosts winning (2–1) but did then pull off a series of great saves in a subsequent friendly against Italy that finished 2–2. He was also busy in a third friendly against Russia which finished 1–1.

As he is only in his early 30s at the time of writing, he looks likely to be in the mix for the 2013 Confederations Cup and the 2014 World Cup in his home country.

Name: Júlio César (Soares Espíndola)
Born: September 3rd 1979, Duque de Caxias
Position: Goalkeeper
International Career: 2003 –
Caps: 67
Goals: 0
Honours: Copa América (2004), Confederations Cup (2009)

Denílson

Denílson made his senior debut for São Paulo aged only 17 in 1994. Four years later Real Betis broke the world record for the highest transfer when they paid £22 million for him. The side was relegated in his second season so he signed for Flamengo on loan for a year. In 2004/05 his goals and assists helped Betis to fourth place in the league (thus qualifying for the Champions League) and the Copa del Rey.

This precociously talented winger first played for Brazil at the age of 19 in 1996. The following year he helped the side win the Copa América and the Confederations Cup and he then played every game at the World Cup, but Brazil could only finish behind hosts France after losing 3-0 in the final.

He made up for the disappointment by joining Luiz Felipe Scolari's squad for the 2002 World Cup in Japan and South Korea. Although he was mostly used as an impact player from the bench, he played in five matches and came on at the end of the final, which Brazil won 2-0 against Germany. Denílson found himself out of favour when Carlos Alberto took over as coach thereafter, however.

Name: Denílson (de Oliveira Araújo)
Born: August 24th 1977, Diadema
Position: Wing
International Career: 1996 – 2003
Caps: 61
Goals: 8
Honours: Copa América (1997), Confederations Cup (1997), World Cup Winner (2002)

Dida

Dida was raised in the small northern Brazilian state of Alagoas and his early heroes were Valdir Peres and Rinat Dasayev. He joined Flamenguinho aged 13 and then his first professional outfit, Cruzeiro, in 1990. Two years later he signed for Vitória and guided them to the state championship. He was then drafted into the national Under-21 squad and helped them to the World Youth Championship.

Having won just about every domestic honour, he moved to Europe in 1999 and joined AC Milan. As he was only the third-choice keeper he was loaned out to SC Corinthians and he helped them to the inaugural World Club Championship after saving several penalties. He was recalled to Milan but his reputation as a fine shot-stopper took a backward step when he fumbled Lee Bowyer's strike at Elland Road in a Champions League fixture against Leeds.

His reputation took another hit when he and several players were found to be in Europe on false Portuguese passports. Milan were heavily fined and Dida was banned for a year. He bounced back with a series of stunning penalty saves to help Milan to the 2003 Champions League trophy, and he was instrumental in the same side winning the Scudetto the following season.

In the 2005 Champions League quarter-final against local rivals Internazionale he was struck by a flare and had to be substituted. The match was eventually abandoned and awarded to Milan as a walkover. In the final against Liverpool, his side blew a 3-0 lead, and his form declined thereafter. Brazilian coach Carlos Alberto Parreira even suggested he might not make the squad for the upcoming World Cup.

Dida's international career had begun a decade earlier when Brazil had beaten Ecuador 1-0, and he was then named as the number-one choice for the 1996 Summer Olympics. He was error-prone at the Games, however, and defeats to Nigeria and Japan meant they could only claim bronze. He helped the side to the Confederations Cup in 1997 and 2005, but he was only on the bench for the 1994 and 2002 World Cup campaigns and played no part in any of the matches.

He was Parreira's pick for the 2006 tournament, however, and he only conceded two goals as Brazil beat Croatia, Australia, Japan and Ghana before being knocked out in the quarter-final by France. In 2006 new coach Dunga dropped him and he couldn't add to his 91 international caps.

He enjoyed a brief resurgence with Milan and lifted the Champions League trophy in 2007, but controversy was never far away. He was tapped on the shoulder by a Celtic fan during their Champions League match in Glasgow in October 2007 and promptly collapsed. Dida was deemed to have faked the injury and was banned for two games. He then suffered a series of injuries and finally left Milan in 2010 for Brazilian club side Portuguesa. In 2012 he joined Grêmio.

Above: *Dida*

Name: Dida (Nélson da Jesus Silva)
Born: October 7th 1973, Irará
Position: Goalkeeper
International Career: 1995 – 2006
Caps: 91
Goals: 0
Honours: Confederations Cup (1997, 2005), Olympic Bronze Medal (1996), World Cup Squad (1994, 2002, 2006)

Didi

Right: *Didi helped Brazil win the World Cup twice*

Didi almost lost his right leg when he picked up a serious infection in his teens, but he recovered and turned professional in 1946. He didn't make much of an impact until he signed for Fluminese in 1949. He missed out on the 1950 World Cup but was selected four years later and he scored goals against Mexico and Yugoslavia before Brazil were beaten by Hungary in the infamous 'Battle of Bern'.

In 1958 he masterminded the first of two Brazilian World Cup triumphs. He was instrumental in the side reaching the final in Sweden and was then voted the best player in the tournament. He was also inspirational in the 1962 event in Chile, scoring several remarkable goals and helping Brazil to consecutive World Cup wins. He retired from international football immediately but he continued his domestic career with Botafogo, Sporting Cristal, São Paulo and CD Veracruz.

He'd first tried management with Cristal in 1962 and he then coached another eight teams – including Peru at the 1970 World Cup – before finally retiring in 1986. Didi was an exquisite footballer with great stamina and flawless technique, and the ability to pick out impossible passes. He also pioneered several different free-kicks with varying amounts of bend and dip.

Name: Didi (Waldyr Pereira)
Born: October 8th 1928, Campos dos Goytacazes
Died: May 12th 2001, Rio de Janeiro
Position: Central midfield
International Career: 1952 - 1962
Caps: 68
Goals: 20
Honours: World Cup Winner (1958, 1962)

Dinamite

Roberto Dinamite began his senior career with Vasco da Gama in 1971. Over the next eight years he would cement his reputation as one of the most feared strikers in the game. Having scored 92 league goals in 161 appearances he joined Barcelona for a year but he returned to Vasco da Gama in 1980 and stayed for another nine years. He eventually became the club's all-time top scorer with 698 (in his entire career he scored 864 goals in 1,022 matches).

Such a talent could not be overlooked by the national selectors and he made his debut in the yellow jersey in 1975 in a 3-1 loss to Peru. He scored his first goal in a 1-0 win over England the following year and was called up for the 1978 World Cup in Argentina. He didn't play in the first two matches but scored the winner against Austria to help Brazil qualify for the second phase. He then scored twice against Poland but Brazil were controversially eliminated on goal difference by the hosts even though they hadn't lost a match.

He was in the squad again four years later but was an unused substitute. He retired from international football in 1984 but continued his domestic career with Vasco da Gama until 1993. He then moved into politics and was elected President of Vasco da Gama in 2008.

Name: Roberto Dinamite (Carlos Roberto de Oliveira)
Born: April 13th 1954, Duque de Caxias
Position: Striker
International Career: 1975 - 1984
Caps: 52
Goals: 27
Honours: World Cup Squad (1978)

Dirceu

Dirceu played for his local side until 1972, and he then signed for Botafogo, Fluminese, Vaso da Gama and América before moving to Europe and joining Atlético Madrid. In only three seasons with the Spanish giants he became a cult hero and scored 18 goals in 84 games.

He enjoyed a long international career in what was a bleak period in Brazilian football. He was first selected in 1973 and made it to the 1974 World Cup, although Brazil could only manage third place. He played again in Argentina four years later and also made it to Spain in 1982. Injury ruled him out of a fourth World Cup at Mexico '86, but by then he'd made 11 World Cup appearances and scored three goals.

Dirceu was a workhorse in the midfield whose lung-busting runs earned him a place in the all-star team for the 1978 World Cup. He was killed in a car crash aged only 43.

Name: Dirceu (José Guimarães)
Born: June 15th 1952, Curitiba
Died: September 15th 1995
Position: Midfield
International Career: 1973 – 1986
Caps: 44
Goals: 7
Honours: World Cup Squad (1974, 1978, 1982)

Dunga

Dunga's uncle nicknamed him 'dopey' because he was short for his age but he eventually grew into a powerful midfielder who signed for various different clubs in his homeland before settling in Fiorentina in 1988. In four seasons with the Italian outfit he made 124 league starts and scored eight goals and he was immediately called up to the national squad.

He had previously captained the Under-20 side at the World Cup and led them to victory over Argentina. Nine years later he was part of the starting XI that performed poorly at Italia '90, and he took a fearful amount of stick from the Brazilian press for his hard-man style of play. But the game was going through a transitional phase and the beautiful Brazilian football of the 1970s and early 1980s was no longer effective against solid Italian defence and German organisation.

Carlos Alberto kept faith with Dunga and awarded him the captaincy during the 1994 World Cup after poor performances from Raí and Mazinho. Despite the low

Above: *Dunga takes control*

quality of the football in the tournament, Brazil stumbled into the final and eventually overcame Italy on penalties. Dunga led the side again four years later but Ronaldo's illness in the build-up to the final against France in Paris clearly affected the team and the hosts cruised to a comfortable win. He retired from the national team after the tournament

but carried on with Júbilo Iwata in Japan before rejoining his first professional club, Internacional. In a playing career spanning two decades, Dunga played more than 500 games and scored nearly 50 goals, not bad for a man criticised as being thuggish and uneasy on the ball.

In 2006 he replaced Carlos Alberto as coach of the national team despite having no experience at this level. He guided Brazil to victory in the 2007 Copa América and 2009 Confederations Cup, but they were beaten by the Netherlands in the quarter-final of the 2010 World Cup in South Africa and Dunga promptly stepped down amidst a storm of criticism. In 2013 he took over as manager of Internacional.

> **Name:** Dunga (Carlos Caetano Bledorn Verri)
> **Born:** October 31st 1963, Ijuí
> **Position:** Defensive midfield
> **International Career:** 1987 - 1998
> **Caps:** 91
> **Goals:** 6
> **Honours:** Olympic Silver Medal (1984), Copa América (1989, 1997), World Cup Winner (1994), Confederations Cup (1997)

Edinho

Edinho was a talented central defender who began his youth career with Fluminese in 1969 at the tender age of 14. He graduated to the senior team in 1975 and made 88 league appearances over the next seven years. He was called up for the national team for the 1976 Summer Olympics in Montreal and again during the qualifying campaign for the 1978 World Cup. He was a regular in the side at the tournament proper, but Brazil were controversially eliminated on goal difference (having not lost a game) after Argentina thrashed Peru 6-0.

He was solid in defence during the 1982 World Cup in Spain when he came on for Serginho in the final group match against minnows New Zealand. Brazil easily qualified for the next phase but he was only on the bench for the crucial second-round match against Argentina, although Brazil won the game comfortably, 3-1. In the next match a Paolo Rossi-inspired Italy knocked them out after an epic encounter. Rossi opened the scoring after five minutes but Sócrates equalised seven minutes later. Rossi netted again after 25 minutes but Falcão levelled for Brazil midway through the second half. Rossi then completed his hat-trick on 74 minutes and won the match for the Italians.

Edinho was captain at the 1986 World Cup in Mexico and they beat Spain in their opening match, Algeria in the next game and Northern Ireland with a wonder goal from Josimar in the last match to finish top of their group. Edinho scored Brazil's third against Poland to put his team in the quarter-final but Sócrates and Júlio César missed their penalties against France in the shootout after the match had ended 1-1 and they were eliminated. It was a disappointing end to what should have been a glittering international career.

Right: *Edinho*

He played on at domestic level with Flamengo, Fluminese and Grêmio before hanging up his boots in 1990. He moved into management immediately but went through 19 clubs over the next 20 years.

Name: Edinho (Edino Nazareth Filho)
Born: June 5th 1955, Rio de Janeiro
Position: Defender
International Career: 1977 – 1986
Caps: 59
Goals: 3
Honours: World Cup Squad (1978, 1982, 1986)

Edmundo

Edmundo was another player who found it difficult to settle at one club. He began his professional career with Vasco da Gama in 1990 but by 2012 he'd played for 13 clubs and never stayed more than two seasons with any of them, although he repeatedly returned to Vasco da Gama. His scoring record is difficult to dispute – he netted 200 goals in 440-odd league appearances – but he was an unusual character who was once prosecuted by animal welfare groups for hiring a circus to perform at his son's first birthday and apparently getting one of the chimps drunk. He then escaped prison after three of his passengers were killed when he was apparently drunk at the wheel.

He was selected for the France '98 World Cup squad and came on for Bebeto against Morocco but he was then an unused sub for the knockout matches against Chile, Denmark and the Netherlands. He made a brief appearance in a losing cause against France in the final but retired two years later when he

Left: *Edmundo*

realised he wasn't going to be picked for the next tournament in the Far East.

Name: Edmundo (Alves de Souza Neto)
Born: April 2nd 1971, Niterói
Position: Striker / wing
International Career: 1992 – 2000
Caps: 39
Goals: 10
Honours: Copa América (1997), World Cup Squad (1998)

Edu

Edu graduated to América's senior team having spent six years in the youth ranks. In eight years with the top-flight outfit he made 402 league appearances and scored 212 goals, an incredible return for a midfielder. Comparisons were being drawn with younger brother Zico (the pair would play together in 1976 at Flamengo) but it was Edu who first broke into the national team at the age of 20. He wasn't selected for the 1970 World Cup in Mexico and missed out again four years later but he was a dribbler of supreme skill who made more than 50 international appearances and scored six goals. He retired in 1981 and immediately moved into coaching with his beloved América. He is now the assistant manager of the Iraqi football team.

Name: Edu (Eduardo Antunes Coimbra)
Born: February 5th 1947, Rio de Janeiro
Position: Attacking midfield
International Career: 1967 – 1974
Caps: 54
Goals: 6
Honours: Copa Rio Branco (1967)

Edú

E dú began his professional career in the Pelé era at Santos. He won five Campeonato Paulista titles between 1967 and 1977 and earned a call-up to the national squad for the 1966 World Cup in England. He didn't make much of an impact initially but he was a regular in the side that won the tournament four years later in Mexico. He won another cap during the disappointing 1974 World Cup and scored eight goals in his international career. He retired from football in the early 1980s but continued to play exhibition matches with his touring all-star masters.

Name: Edú (Jonas Eduardo Américo)
Born: August 6th 1949, Jaú
Position: Midfield
International Career: 1966 – 1976
Caps: 45
Goals: 8
Honours: World Cup Winner (1970)

Elano

Elano's senior career began with Santos, for whom he made 129 league appearances and scored 34 goals between 2001 and 2004. This talented midfielder soon attracted the attention of club sides in Europe and he signed for Ukrainian side Shakhtar Donetsk for the next three years. During this spell he was called up to the national team and he scored his first goals against Argentina in a friendly at Arsenal's Emirates Stadium in 2006. He didn't make it to the World Cup later that year but became a regular thereafter and helped the team win the Copa América in 2007 and the Confederations Cup two years later.

He was in the national squad for the 2010 World Cup in South Africa and he scored against North Korea and the Ivory Coast, although he then picked up an injury and played no further part in the tournament. His domestic career continued with Manchester City, Galatasaray and Santos before he joined Grêmio in 2012.

Name: Elano (Blumer)
Born: June 14th 1981, Iracemápolis
Position: Midfield
International Career: 2004 – 2011
Caps: 50
Goals: 9
Honours: Copa América (2007), Confederations Cup (2009)

Émerson

Émerson joined club side Comercial in 1968 and was so impressive in his first two seasons that he was called up to the national squad as a reserve before the 1970 World Cup in Mexico. He made two appearances but didn't cement his place in the side until the 1974 tournament. Brazil squeezed through their qualifying round on goals scored after three draws. They then edged out East Germany 1-0 and Argentina 2-1 to face the Netherlands in what had effectively become a semi-final. This was a time when the Dutch were masters of total football, however, and goals from Johan Neeskens and Johan Cruyff put Brazil out. They were then beaten by Poland in the third-place match.

Four years later Émerson became the first goalkeeper to captain the national team at the 1978 World Cup in Argentina but the tournament was a disappointment for Brazil. They could only draw with Spain and Sweden, even though a last-minute Zico header should have given them victory over the Swedes. Welsh referee Clive Thomas controversially blew for full-time before the ball crossed the line, however, and the goal didn't stand. They did manage to beat Austria in their final group game but they only finished second in that group.

There was more controversy in the second round. Brazil beat Peru 3-0 and Poland 3-1, while Argentina beat Poland 2-0 and then drew with Brazil. This left Argentina needing to beat Peru by four clear goals to progress at Brazil's expense. Rumours have circulated ever since their ridiculously easy 6-0 win that the Peruvian team were bribed to throw the game, but nothing was ever proved. Brazil saw off Italy in the third-place match and were dubbed the moral champions because they hadn't lost a game during the tournament.

Émerson missed out on the 1982 World Cup and could only make the reserves' bench in 1986. Having retired he moved straight into management. He enjoyed some success at club level

Above: *Émerson Leão*

and then coached the national team in 2000/01. Of his 11 matches in charge, Brazil won four, drew four and lost three. His tenure with club sides and the national team was always controversial and he flitted between 29 sides between 1987 and 2012.

Name: Émerson Leão
Born: July 11th 1949, Ribeirão Preto
Position: Goalkeeper
International Career: 1969 – 1986
Caps: 80
Goals: 0
Honours: World Cup Winner (1970)

Fabiano

Luís Fabiano began his senior career with Ponte Preta in 1998. He then moved to Rennes, although he went back to Brazil for a loan year with São Paulo, before signing with the Brazilian club for another two years. He hadn't enjoyed a great return in front of goal until that point, but his 52 goals in 65 league appearances announced him on the world stage. He then joined Porto for a season before settling at Sevilla for six years, during which time he won the UEFA Cup. In his next 149 league games he scored an incredible 72 goals and cemented his place in the national team.

He'd first been selected for a friendly against Nigeria and marked his debut with a goal, and he and Adriano then ran the line during the glorious 2004 Copa América campaign. However, a run of poor form with Porto and Sevilla kept him out of the reckoning for another three years. He then won the Golden Boot during the 2009 Confederations Cup and was selected for the 2010 World Cup in South Africa. He scored three goals in the tournament but couldn't help Brazil past the quarter-final and he wasn't picked again until 2012.

He is still showing good form for São Paulo and looks likely to feature at his home World Cup in 2014.

Above: *Luís Fabiano*

Name: Luís Fabiano (Clemente Palomino)
Born: November 8th 1980, Campinas
Position: Striker
International Career: 2003 –
Caps: 45
Goals: 28
Honours: Copa América (2004), Confederations Cup (2009)

Falcão

Falcão joined Internacional in his home country in 1972. In the next eight years he played 158 league games, scored 22 goals and won three national championships (1975, 1976 and 1979). A big-money move to Roma followed where he was even better, scoring another 22 league goals in 107 games. They would have won the 1980/81 Scudetto had Roma not had a goal ruled out against Juventus but Falcão had to make do with the Coppa Italia instead.

He inexplicably missed out on selection for the 1978 World Cup but by 1982 he was one of the finest midfielders in the world and could not be ignored for the World Cup in Spain. His goals were vital in Brazil's matches against the Soviet Union and New Zealand, and he then helped them overcome archrivals Argentina. Despite only needing a draw against Italy to progress to the semi-final, Paolo Rossi's unforgettable hat-trick meant that Falcão was a devastated member of one of the best teams never to have won the tournament. In fact he was so distressed after the match – in which he had scored the second equaliser only for Rossi to score a late

winner – that he vowed to retire.

He was past his best at the 1986 World Cup in Mexico and had probably been picked on reputation and ability rather than form. He only played in two of the matches (as a sub against Spain and Algeria) and he retired after Brazil's exit to a Platini-inspired France in the quarter-final. Indeed he, Liam Brady and Platini were the three big foreign stars in Serie A for the next four years, although Falcão left Europe after an unauthorised knee operation and returned to Brazil to coach. He briefly took the reins of the national team after the 1990 World Cup but he achieved little and retired after managing Japan for a year in 1994. He returned to management in 2011 with Internacional, however.

Name: (Paulo Roberto) Falcão
Born: October 16th 1953, Abelardo Luz
Position: Midfield
International Career: 1976 - 1986
Caps: 34
Goals: 7
Honours: World Cup Squad (1982, 1986)

Félix

Félix began his career with club side Atlético Juventus in São Paulo in 1951. He moved between several domestic outfits before returning to Portuguesa in 1958. He remained with the club for a decade, during which he won his first international cap in 1965. Three years later he joined Fluminese, and several solid performances saw him selected for the 1970 World Cup in Mexico. His spectacular point-blank save from Francis Lee saw Brazil edge out England in their second match, 1-0. Although he was an acrobatic shot-stopper, Félix was prone to positional errors and tactical blunders, and there's no doubt he enjoyed his fair share of luck, but he managed to keep his place as Brazil beat Czechoslovakia, Romania, Peru, Uruguay and then Italy in the final to lift the trophy for the third time.

He won the last of his international caps in 1972, although he played on for Fluminese for another four years and secured his fifth state title in 1976. Having retired, he briefly turned his hand to

coaching but he contracted emphysema after a lifetime of heavy smoking and died in 2012.

Above: *Félix is carried aloft at the end of the 1970 World Cup final*

Name: Félix (Félix Miélli Venerando)
Born: December 24th 1937
Died: August 24th 2012
Position: Goalkeeper
International Career: 1965 – 1972
Caps: 47
Goals: 0
Honours: World Cup Winner (1970)

Fred

Right: *Fred pulls on the yellow of Brazil*

Fred had a long youth career with América Mineiro and he graduated to the senior team in 2002. He scored one of the fastest goals in history (3.17 seconds after kick-off) against São Paulo and has consistently found the net for all of his senior clubs: 24 goals in 43 league games for Cruzeiro, 34 in 88 games for Lyon, and 59 in 87 league starts for Fluminese. It was this form that saw him picked for Brazil's friendly against Guatemala in 2005.

Despite not playing any part in Brazil's qualifying campaign, he was selected for the 2006 World Cup in Germany, and he scored his first goal against Australia in the group stage. The tournament was a disappointment, however, with Brazil being eliminated in the quarter-final. Although he bounced back to form in the following year's Copa América, Fred found it difficult to cement a place in the starting XI. He was eventually recalled by returning coach Luiz Felipe Scolari on the back of solid domestic performances in 2013 and he repaid the faith by scoring against England at Wembley. He should feature at the 2014 World Cup if he can stay fit and continue scoring for Fluminese.

Name: Fred (Frederico Chaves Guedes)
Born: October 3rd 1983, Teofilo Otoni
Position: Striker
International Career: 2005 –
Caps: 22
Goals: 10
Honours: Copa América (2007), Superclásico de las Américas (2011, 2012)

Friedenreich

Arthur Friedenreich was born to a German businessman and an African–Brazilian washerwoman. He developed into a player of great skill, sublime finishing and a deft touch. He would eventually become the first black superstar even though he initially faced stiff opposition from the establishment in a sport that was run by whites and predominantly played by the white upper classes. He began playing with teams of German immigrants but was so good that he could no longer be overlooked by the national team and he made his debut in 1914.

He helped Brazil to the Copa América in 1919 and 1922 and became known as 'The King' on a tour to Europe three years later. He didn't make it into the squad for the 1930 World Cup because of a misunderstanding between the leagues in Rio de Janeiro and São Paulo, and by 1934 he was too old to be considered. He retired from domestic football aged 43 after the 1935 season with Flamengo.

Although the goal-scorers in some

games weren't recorded, and many match reports were inaccurate, most reliable sources credit this incredible player with 1395 goals from only 1239 games (1909-1935), statistics that are virtually unmatched in world sport and unapproachable in the modern game.

Name: Arthur Friedenreich
Born: July 18th 1892, São Paulo
Died: September 6th 1969, São Paulo
Position: Striker
International Career: 1914 – 1925
Caps: 23
Goals: 10
Honours: Copa América (1919, 1922)

Garrincha

Garrincha was born with severe birth defects – a curved spine, twisted right leg and a left leg six centimetres shorter and curved outwards – to an alcoholic father, but he was determined to make it as a professional footballer. He was married and with a child before he had a trial with Botafogo, however. He was such a technically gifted player that Nilton Santos insisted the club hire him and he also put him forward for the national team. Garrincha scored a hat-trick on his professional debut but couldn't break into the Brazilian team for the 1954 World Cup because the selectors went with Julinho. His club career would go from strength to strength however: over the next 12 years he made 581 appearances for Botafogo and scored 232 goals.

He was picked for the 1958 World Cup in Sweden on the back of his outstanding form and he repeatedly terrorised defenders with his pace and skill. He set up the first two goals in the final and was named in the team of the tournament. His career then took a bizarre turn: he was dropped for a friendly against England because of his drinking, then he got a local girl pregnant when touring in Sweden, and when he returned home he ran his father over while both were drunk. His father died in 1959 from liver cancer.

When Pelé picked up an injury at the 1962 World Cup, Garrincha assumed the mantle and guided the team to the final (he'd been sent off in the semi against hosts Chile because he'd retaliated after being repeatedly fouled, but he wasn't suspended). He was voted player of the tournament after a 3-1 win over Czechoslovakia. He played his last international match against Hungary during the 1966 World Cup. It was the only match Brazil lost while he was playing.

His personal life was in stark contrast to his glittering football

career. He was involved in many road accidents, one of which killed his mother-in-law, and he fathered at least 14 children by four women. He died a forgotten hero in 1983 after being hospitalised eight times with severe alcoholism. He was then voted one of the three greatest forwards of the 20th century.

Name: Garrincha (Manuel Francisco dos Santos)
Born: October 28th 1933, Pau Grande
Died: January 20th 1983, Rio de Janeiro
Position: Wing
International Career: 1955 – 1966
Caps: 50
Goals: 12
Honours: World Cup Winner (1958, 1962)

Gérson

Gérson's father and uncle were professional footballers, and his heroes as a boy were Zizinho, Ademir and Danilo. He was a player of some talent and signed for Flamengo in 1959. In the next four years he played 153 league matches and scored 80 goals, most of which with his devastating left foot. He had the ability to read and control the game from midfield and he was soon called up to the national team. Were it not for a serious knee injury, he would surely have partnered Garrincha, Pelé and Didi to World Cup glory in Chile in 1962. Four years later he had a poor tournament in England but he was at his peak for Mexico '70.

As one of the greatest passers and tacticians, Gérson masterminded Brazil's victory and he scored in the final against Italy. And as he was the standout player in the tournament, it came as something of a surprise when Pelé overlooked him in his list of 125 greatest footballers. His 14 goals in 70 Brazilian starts and 207 goals in 603 games overall suggest he was easily good enough to make the grade.

Name: Gérson (de Oliveira Nunes)
Born: January 11th 1941, Niterói
Position: Playmaker
International Career: 1961 – 1972
Caps: 70
Goals: 14
Honours: World Cup Winner (1970)

Gilmar

Gilmar was apparently named after his parents (Gilberto and Maria) and he began his career with Jabaquara in 1945. Six years later he signed for Corninthians and he promptly secured three state championships in 1951, 1952 and 1954. He was called up by the national team in 1953 but wasn't the first choice keeper for the following year's World Cup in Switzerland and instead had to wait until 1958 in Sweden.

Brazil could only draw 0-0 with England but they then beat Austria 3-0 and the Soviet Union 2-0 to qualify top of their group. In the quarter-final they squeezed past Wales before a Pelé hat-trick saw them beat France comfortably in the semi-final, 5-2. They won the final by the same score-line against hosts Sweden with a brace from Pelé and Vavá and a single goal from future coach Mário Zagallo.

Four years later Gilmar was again the number one keeper in Brazil and he started every game at the World Cup in Chile. They opened the tournament with a 2-0 win over Mexico but could then only draw 0-0 with Czechoslovakia. They topped the group after a 2-1 victory over Spain, however. In the knockout stages Gilmar was beaten four times but his team-mates managed to score three against England, four against Chile and another three against Czechoslovakia in the final. Gilmar therefore became the only goalkeeper to date to win consecutive World Cups.

He was selected for the World Cup in England in 1966 but the tournament was a disappointment: their opponents targeted Pelé with some merciless tackling and effectively kicked him out of the event. Brazil did manage to overcome Bulgaria but they were then soundly beaten by Hungary and Portugal and were eliminated.

He'd switched domestic clubs to Santos in 1961 and he enjoyed another

eight years with the all-conquering outfit. His form remained good so he was still with the national squad until 1969, when he retired from football. In all he racked up 752 domestic appearances and 94 international caps. He was then voted the best Brazilian goalkeeper of the 20th century.

Name: Gilmar (Gylmar dos Santos Neves)
Born: August 22nd 1930, Santos
Position: Goalkeeper
International Career: 1953 – 1969
Caps: 94
Goals: 0
Honours: World Cup Winner (1958, 1962)

Gomes

Ricardo Gomes began his professional career with Fluminese in 1982. Over the next six years he racked up more than 200 league appearances and 11 goals. In 1988 he moved to Europe and joined Benfica, and in three years he made 83 league appearances, scored another 19 goals and, along with compatriot Valdo, guided the side to the title in 1988 and 1991.

He was called up by Brazil in 1984 and was a regular fixture in the team for the next decade. He helped an inexperienced side to the silver medal at the 1988 Seoul Olympics and played in every match at the 1990 World Cup in Italy. His power in the air, pace and superb distribution helped Brazil overcome Sweden, Costa Rica and Scotland. However solid the team was defensively though, it lacked firepower upfront and this shortcoming would come back to haunt the side in the last 16 when they were knocked out by archrivals and eventual finalists Argentina. The game was also notable for Gomes's red card in the 85th minute of a bruising encounter in Turin.

The national selectors stood by him, however, and he was chosen to captain Brazil at the 1994 World Cup in the USA. Gomes missed the tournament (and therefore a winners' medal) having picked up a serious injury beforehand. He retired from international football immediately but played on at club level with Paris Saint-Germain and Benfica.

In 1996 he moved into management and he has so far coached Recife, Fluminese, Flamengo, Bordeaux, Monaco, São Paulo and Vasco da Gama.

Name: Ricardo Gomes (Raimundo)
Born: December 13th 1964, Rio de Janeiro
Position: Defender
International Career: 1984 – 1994
Caps: 45
Goals: 4
Honours: Copa América (1989), World Cup Squad (1990)

Guia

Right: Domingos da Guia

Domingos da Guia began playing with local side Bangu at the age of 17, and he then graduated to Flamengo via Nacional, Vasco da Gama and Boca Juniors. He immediately established himself in the centre of defence and was given the nickname 'The Divine Master'. He came to international prominence at the World Cup in 1938 and helped the side to the semi-final after wins over Poland and Czechoslovakia.

He then joined Corinthians but the Second World War prevented him from adding to his appearances for Brazil. He eventually retired with 30 international caps as one of the greatest players in Flamengo and Corinthian history, and one of the best defenders the world game has yet seen.

Name: Domingos (Antônio) da Guia
Born: November 19th 1912, Rio de Janeiro
Died: May 18th 2000, Rio de Janeiro
Position: Defender
International Career: 1931 – 1946
Caps: 30
Goals: 0
Honours: World Cup Squad (1938)

Hulk

Hulk was given his nickname by his father, who was a fan of the TV show. His professional career kicked off with Vitória but he moved to Kawasaki Frontale in Japan for a season-long loan and then two further seasons. He didn't get much game time until he joined Consadole Sapporo and Tokyo Verdy, when he managed 69 goals in 93 league appearances. This was enough to interest several European clubs and he signed for Porto in 2008. Another successful stint (54 goals in 99 starts) saw him called up to the national team.

It took him three years to score his first international goals (a brace against Denmark), but he was then selected as one of the three overage players at the 2012 London Olympics. He scored in the final against Mexico but couldn't prevent Brazil losing 2-1. Hulk is another young player who should feature in Mano Menezes's Brazil side in the build-up to the 2014 World Cup.

Name: Hulk (Givanildo Vieira de Souza)
Born: July 25th 1986, Campina Grande
Position: Striker
International Career: 2009 –
Caps: 20
Goals: 6
Honours: Olympic Silver Medal (2012)

Above: *Hulk unleashes a long ball with his left foot*

Jair

Right: *Jair was one of the finest footballers of his generation*

Jair began his career on the wing for Madureira in 1938 and he was so good that he made his debut for the national team two years later. He scored the only Brazilian goal in a humiliating 6-1 defeat to Argentina, but he then scored a hat-trick against Uruguay. Two more goals in a 7-0 annihilation of Paraguay helped the side to the Copa América in 1949.

The following year Brazil played beautiful samba football and scored 22 goals in their first six World Cup matches. Jair, Ademir and Zizinho were the stars of an exceptional team so it came as something of a shock when they were beaten by Uruguay in the de facto final. The Defeat, as it is now known, was so embedded on the national psyche that Brazil changed to yellow shirts in future, and Jair, who'd hit the post in the match, said afterwards: "I'll take that loss to my grave."

The selectors needed a scapegoat and Jair, shamefully, wasn't picked again until 1956, although by then he was past his best and only managed another two games.

He finally retired from domestic football in 1963 and moved into management. While at Santos he helped nurture and mentor a young player who would go on to great things. His name was Edson Arantes do Nascimento. We know him better as Pelé.

Jair died from a lung infection aged 84 in 2005.

Name: Jair (da Rosa Pinto)
Born: March 21st 1921, Quatis
Died: July 28th 2005, Rio de Janeiro
Position: Attacking midfield
International Career: 1940 - 1956
Caps: 49
Goals: 22
Honours: Copa América (1949), World Cup Runner-up (1950)

Jairzinho

Jairzinho joined youth team Botafogo and made his professional debut for the senior team at the age of 15. He couldn't play in his preferred position initially because Garrincha played on the right so he switched to the left and made an immediate impact. He resisted the temptation to move to Europe and spent 15 glorious years with Botafogo, making 413 league appearances and scoring 186 goals, an incredible return for a midfielder, albeit one who bombed forward at every opportunity to whip in devilish crosses or to shoot.

He made his debut for the national team when Garrincha was injured in 1964, but he couldn't help the side past the opening round at the 1966 World Cup in England. When Garrincha retired, Jairzinho switched back to the right and became the legendary 'Hurricane' at the 1970 World Cup in Mexico. He scored in every match of the tournament, one of only three players ever to do so (the others being Uruguay's Alcides Ghiggia in 1950 and France's Just Fontaine in 1958), although he didn't win the Golden Boot as Germany's Gerd Müller scored ten to his seven.

He scored another two goals at the 1974 World Cup but he couldn't guide the side to the final and they bowed out in the play-off for third place. Jairzinho's domestic career wound down over the same period and, although he continued for a number of clubs, he never stayed more than a season or two and finally hung up his boots after a farewell international in 1982. He returned to football 20 years later as manager of Gabon.

He continues to be revered as a player and is consistently voted one of the top 30 players of all time. He is also credited with spotting Ronaldo as a 14-year-old and recommending him to Cruzeiro. Ronaldo would go on to become one of the game's modern greats and a three-time World Player of the Year.

Above: *Jairzinho at the 1974 World Cup*

Name: Jairzinho (Jair Ventura Filho)
Born: December 25th 1944, Rio de Janeiro
Position: Wing
International Career: 1964 – 1982
Caps: 81
Goals: 33
Honours: World Cup Winner (1970)

Jorginho

Below: *Jorginho at the 1994 World Cup in the USA*

Jorginho began his professional career with América of Rio de Janeiro but he signed for Flamengo after two years and 20 appearances. He stayed for five years and racked up 188 starts and seven goals. He also won his first international cap at the Rous Cup in 1987. He was then elected for the 1988 Summer Olympics in Seoul, South Korea, and helped his side to the final, although they lost 2-1 to the Soviet Union.

He was also picked for the 1990 World Cup in Italy but the tournament was a disappointment and Brazil failed to live up to their high expectations. Four years later much of the same team made amends at the tournament in the United States. Jorginho played in every match and, despite picking up an injury 20 minutes into the final against Italy, he was named in the all-star team of the tournament. Roberto Baggio's missed penalty at the end of a dour final meant that Brazil were crowned World Champions, although Jorginho's international career then began a slow decline and he was eventually replaced by Cafu.

After successful spells with Bayer Leverkusen and Bayern Munich, Jorginho returned to Brazil and carried on playing with various clubs until 2002, although by then he was well past his best and only managed 45 appearances in four seasons. In 2006 he turned his hand to managing, first with América and then as assistant to Dunga with the national team. After a poor showing at the 2010 World Cup, both Jorginho and Dunga left, with the former reverting to club management in his home country.

Name: Jorginho (Jorge de Amorim Campos)
Born: August 17th 1964, Rio de Janeiro
Position: Right back
International Career: 1987 – 1995
Caps: 64
Goals: 3
Honours: Rous Cup (1987), Olympic Silver Medal (1988), Copa América (1989), World Cup Winner (1994)

Juan

Juan began his career at Flamengo but he didn't see much first-team action and only averaged 12 appearances per season. In 2002 he signed for German giants Bayer Leverkusen and eventually racked up 139 league appearances and 10 goals. The move also saw him recognised by the national team and he collected the Copa América and Confederations Cups twice each. He also scored against Chile to help Brazil into the quarter-final of the 2010 World Cup, although they were then eliminated by the Netherlands.

Juan left Leverkusen in 2007 for Roma and stayed with the Italian Serie A side for the next six seasons. He made more than 140 starts and scored 11 goals in all competitions but by then he was past his best, and he made his last appearance for Brazil in the World Cup defeat to the Dutch.

Left: *Juan*

Name: Juan (Silveira dos Santos)
Born: February 1st 1979, Rio de Janeiro
Position: Defender
International Career: 2001 – 2010
Caps: 79
Goals: 7
Honours: Copa América (2004, 2007),
Confederations Cup (2005, 2009)

Julinho

Julinho was a naturally gifted player who used great pace to torment the opposition down the flanks. He began his domestic career with Portuguesa but soon signed for Fluminese and then Palmeiras. He transferred to Italian giants Fiorentina and won the Scudetto in 1956 but he couldn't help the side win the European Championship the following year because they came up against Real Madrid in the final. He was voted the club's best player of all time in 1996, however.

He'd first been called up by Brazil in time for the 1954 World Cup and he impressed at the tournament by scoring goals against Mexico in their opening game and Hungary in the ill-tempered quarter-final that saw Brazil eliminated after a 4–2 defeat.

Name: Julinho (Júlio Botelho)
Born: July 29th 1929, São Paulo
Died: January 10th 2003
Position: Wing
International Career: 1952 – 1965
Caps: 25
Goals: 13
Honours: World Cup Squad (1954)

Juninho

Juninho began his professional career with São Paulo – where he won four trophies in two years – but he then made a surprise move to Middlesbrough in 1995. The diminutive playmaker made an immediate impact on English football and he helped the Teessiders to the 1997 League Cup and FA Cup finals, although they lost them both and were then relegated.

He was desperate to play for the national side so he signed for Atlético Madrid for £12 million, but his career was hampered by injuries and he missed the 1998 World Cup with a broken leg. He was in the Brazil squad for the victorious 2002 campaign in the Far East but, when he returned to Middlesbrough and helped them to the 2004 League Cup, he said the latter victory was more important that winning the World Cup with the national team.

He retired from international football in 2003 with 49 caps and five goals under his belt but he continued playing domestically until 2010. On the last day of the season he scored the goal that saved his club side Ituano from relegation.

Above: *Juninho outmanoeuvres the German defence in the (2002) World Cup final*

Name: Juninho (Osvaldo Giroldo Júnior)
Born: February 22nd 1973, São Paulo
Position: Attacking midfield
International Career: 1995 – 2003
Caps: 49
Goals: 5
Honours: Confederations Cup (1997), World Cup Winner 2002

Júnior, Leovegildo

Júnior was a prodigiously talented two-footed defender who could also play on the left side of midfield. He joined Flamengo in 1974 and remained with the club for a decade before signing for Torino and Pescara.

He then rejoined Flamengo in 1989 to see out his domestic career with his home team. In his time with them, he won four Brazilian Championships and both the Copa Libertadores and Intercontinental Cups in 1981. His total of 857 club appearances is also a record.

In 1979 he was called up to the national squad in the wake of their elimination from the World Cup in Argentina, and was a regular in the team for the next 13 years. Pelé

voted him one of his top 125 living footballers in 2004 for his versatility, technique and tireless teamwork. He was picked for the 1982 and 1986 World Cups, although he couldn't help a star-studded team win the greatest prize.

He retired from both domestic and international football in 1992 but returned the following year to coach Flamengo. He then had a brief stint managing Corinthians. He is also a huge draw at the Beach Soccer World Cup, scoring vital goals and being voted the player of the tournament.

Name: Júnior (Leovegildo Lins da Gama Júnior)
Born: June 29th 1954, João Pessoa
Position: Defender
International Career: 1979 – 1992
Caps: 74
Goals: 9
Honours: World Cup Squad (1982, 1986), Copa América Runner-up (1983)

Júnior, Roque

Roque Júnior began his career at Santarritense but he moved to São José for one season before settling at Palmeiras in 1995. He made 192 league appearances for the club and scored 15 goals and earned a call-up to the national squad in the wake of the World Cup final defeat to France in 1998. At the next tournament in the Far East, Brazil swept Turkey, China and Costa Rica aside, although Roque Júnior only played in the first two matches. He was back in the starting line-up for the first knockout match against Belgium, which they won 2-0, and he was also in the team that beat England in the quarter-final. He was instrumental in quelling a number of Turkish attacks in the semi-final and he also started the final against Germany.

He was still with the team for their Confederations Cup success in 2005 but he was injured for the defence of the World Cup in Germany and was past his best anyway. He retired from international football in 2007 as one of the most respected defenders in the game.

His domestic career had seen several ups and downs, and Peter Reid somehow convinced him to join Leeds United on loan in 2003 after he'd enjoyed three successful years with Italian giants Milan. He only made seven appearances in the UK and the side conceded 24 goals. He was sent off on his debut against Birmingham but did then score twice in a losing cause against Manchester United in a Worthington Cup tie.

He then had four seasons in Germany before returning to Brazil with Palmeiras. He retired from all football in 2010 but does occasionally coach São José's youth side.

Above: *Roque Júnior takes to the air*

> **Name:** (José Vito) Roque Júnior
> **Born:** August 31st 1976, Santa Rita
> **Position:** Defender
> **International Career:** 1999 – 2005
> **Caps:** 50
> **Goals:** 2
> **Honours:** World Cup Winner (2002), Confederations Cup (2005)

Kaká

Kaká was born into an affluent family that allowed him to concentrate on football and schoolwork equally. He had six productive years with youth club São Paulo, although his career was almost ended when he fractured his spine. He graduated to the senior team in 2001 and scored 23 goals in 59 appearances. Several top European clubs tried to sign him and he eventually chose Milan. He won the Scudetto and UEFA Super Cup in his first season. Milan recovered from the agony of losing the 2005 Champions League final to Liverpool and avenged the defeat two years later. He was consistently voted Europe's best playmaker and he contributed vital goals in the 2007 season when he also won the Ballon d'Or.

Two years later, Manchester City reportedly made a world-record bid of £100 million for Kaká. Silvio Berlusconi convinced him to stay but he signed for Real Madrid in the summer for around £60 million. A knee injury kept him on the sidelines for four months but he soon became an integral member of the team alongside Cristiano Ronaldo, Karim Benzema, Pepe and Iker Casillas.

He has been equally impressive on the international stage since earning his first cap in 2002. He was part of the

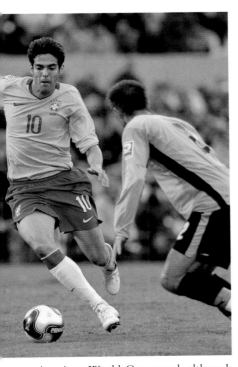

World Cup, but the tournament was a disappointment and they bowed out after defeat to France.

Kaká was voted the best player of the tournament during the 2009 Confederations Cup but he was then sent off in Brazil's game against the Ivory Coast at the 2010 World Cup in South Africa. He spent the next year on the sidelines and only returned in 2011 but he then picked up an injury and didn't play until 2012. Luiz Felipe Scolari stood by him and selected him for two friendlies in early 2013 and if he can stay fit he might just make Brazil's squad for their home World Cup.

victorious World Cup squad, although he only played 25 minutes against Costa Rica, but then he cemented his place in the side after victory over Argentina in the 2005 Confederations Cup. He was man of the match in Brazil's opener against Croatia at the 2006

Name: Kaká (Ricardo Izecson dos Santos Leite)
Born: April 22nd 1982, Gama
Position: Attacking midfield
International Career: 2002 –
Caps: 87
Goals: 29
Honours: World Cup Winner (2002), Confederations Cup (2005, 2009)

Leonardo

Leonardo began his professional career with Flamengo alongside Zico, Leandro, Bebeto and Renato in 1987. He signed for São Paulo, Valencia, Kashima Antlers and Paris Saint-Germain before settling in Italy with Milan for four years. He made 177 appearances and scored 25 goals and was called up for the national team for the 1994 World Cup in the USA. He kept Roberto Carlos out of the team for the group matches but was then banned for the remainder of the tournament after elbowing American midfielder Tab Ramos. Ramos's injuries were so severe that he was hospitalised for more than three months.

Leonardo inherited the number ten shirt thereafter and was a key member of the side that reached the final of the next World Cup in France. Ronaldo's illness diverted the team's attention and they lost to the hosts 3-0. He played his last international during qualifying for the 2002 World Cup in Japan and Korea and eventually racked up 60 appearances and eight goals.

He retired from domestic football the following year and worked briefly as a pundit with the BBC before turning his attention to scouting and acting as an agent. In 2009 he took over from Carlo Ancelotti as manager of Milan, although he crossed the city to join archrivals Internazionale the following season. He joined Ancelotti at Paris Saint-Germain in 2011.

Name: Leonardo (Nascimento de Araújo)
Born: September 5th 1969, Niterói
Position: Attacking midfield / left back
International Career: 1990 – 2002
Caps: 60
Goals: 8
Honours: World Cup Winner (1994), Copa América (1997)

Leônidas

Leônidas was one of the greatest pre-war players and his goal-scoring records may never be matched. He began his career in 1929 with São Cristóvão and in one exceptional season he scored 31 goals in 29 games. He continued this trend of scoring at better than a goal a game until 1942, racking up an incredible 313 goals in his next 301 league starts.

This form saw him selected for the 1934 World Cup in Italy but he only played in one match (against Spain), although he did score Brazil's only goal. Four years later he dominated the tournament in France, scoring three against Poland, two against Czechoslovakia and another two against Sweden in the third-place match. The war robbed him off his best years and he retired from international football in 1946 with 21 goals in only 19 appearances.

This incomparable genius is credited with inventing the bicycle kick, scoring the only such goal during the World Cup, and then repeating the effort in an 8-0

Above: *Leônidas da Silva is credited with perfecting the bicycle kick*

demolition of Juventus in 1948 that so shocked the referee that he didn't know whether to allow the goal to stand.

He rounded off his domestic career in style with São Paulo, scoring another 140 league goals in 211 appearances between 1943 and 1950. He briefly managed the side after his retirement but fell ill in 1973 with Alzheimer's. He battled the disease for 30 years before passing away in 2004.

Name: Leônidas (da Silva)
Born: September 6th 1913, Rio de Janeiro
Died: January 24th 2004, Cotia
Position: Striker
International Career: 1932 - 1946
Caps: 19
Goals: 21
Honours: World Cup Squad (1934, 1938 – third place)

Love

Vágner Love began his senior career with Palmeiras in 2002 and he scored 27 league goals in 42 games during his first two seasons. He came to the attention of CSKA Moscow and signed for the club in 2004, returning another 79 goals in 158 league starts and helping the team to the UEFA Cup, the Russian League, two Russian Cups and the Super Cup. It was this form that brought him into the national team, and he made his debut in 2004. Over the next three years he played 26 times for the Seleção (the nickname for the national team) and scored nine goals but he couldn't cement a place in the starting line-up.

He rejoined Palmeiras on loan in 2009 and then Flamengo the following season, before returning to Moscow in 2013. He is a potent attacking weapon with great stamina, flair and precise finishing but he will have to up his game if he wants to be selected for the 2014 World Cup in Brazil.

Name: Vágner (Silva de Souza) Love
Born: June 11th 1984, Rio de Janeiro
Position: Striker
International Career: 2004 – 2007
Caps: 26
Goals: 9
Honours: Copa América (2004, 2007)

Lúcio

Lúcio began his junior career with his local club but he signed for Internacional in 1998. He earned more than 50 caps and negotiated a move to Bayer Leverkusen in 2001. The club were just pipped to the Bundesliga title by Borussia Dortmund and they also lost in the cup final to Schalke 04. Their third major defeat happened on an even bigger stage – the Champions League final – when a wonder goal from Zinedine Zidane won the trophy for Real Madrid. Lúcio's sterling performances included a goal in the CL final and several top European clubs opened their chequebooks in the hope of securing his signature. A deal to Roma fell through so he moved to Bayern Munich instead.

He was an integral cog in the defence alongside Dutchman Mark van Bommel but the side couldn't get past the quarter-finals in the Champions League. He then transferred to Internazionale and sealed a historic treble with a 2-0 win over Bayern in the Champions League final. He then had a brief stint with Juventus before returning to Brazil and joining São Paulo.

Lúcio enjoyed an 11-year international career having first been called up for Brazil in 2000. It was his mistake that allowed Michael Owen to score for England in their quarter-final at the 2002 World Cup but goals from Ronaldinho and Rivaldo ensured Brazil progressed. They knocked out Turkey in the semi-final and overcame Germany in the final. Only Lúcio, Cafu and Marcos played every minute of every game.

Brazil had a poor tournament in 2006 so new coach Dunga named Lúcio as his captain in the aftermath, and it was his header in the 84th minute of the 2009 Confederations Cup that sealed victory for

LÚCIO

Right: *Lúcio and Scotland's Kenny Miller jostle for position in 2010*

Brazil over the USA. Lúcio then captained the side at the 2010 World Cup. Brazil qualified comfortably from their group but they could only beat Chile in the last 16 and went out to the Dutch in the quarter-final. A strong presence at the back and solid in the air and in attack, Lúcio played his last international in 2011.

Name: Lúcio (Lucimar Ferreira da Silva)
Born: May 8th 1978, Planaltina
Position: Central Defender
International Career: 2000 – 2011
Caps: 105
Goals: 4
Honours: World Cup Winner (2002), Confederations Cup (2005, 2009)

Luisinho

Luisinho developed into one of the most feared pre-war strikers. He enjoyed an 18-year career with a number of clubs although he is most closely associated with São Paulo and Palmeiras, for whom he won seven state championships and scored 268 league goals between 1930 and 1947.

He first represented Brazil in the 1934 World Cup against Spain, and he then scored five goals during the 1937 South American Championship. He was again picked for the World Cup squad in 1938, although he only managed two appearances. He was another player whose career was interrupted by the war, and he retired in 1944 at the age of 33.

Name: Luisinho (Luís Mesquita de Oliveira)
Born: March 29th 1911, Rio de Janeiro
Died: December 27th 1983, São Paulo
Position: Striker
International Career: 1934 – 1944
Caps: 9
Goals: 5
Honours: World Cup Squad (1934, 1938)

Left: *Luisinho was one of the deadliest pre-war strikers*

Luiz

Right: *David Luiz*

David Luiz was released by the youth team of São Paulo FC when he was 14 but he was snapped up by Vitória in 2001. He stayed with the club for his first two professional years before moving to Europe and joining Benfica on loan. The loan deal became permanent in 2007, and by 2011 he'd notched up 72 league appearances and four goals, as well as the 2009/10 Portuguese title and the League Cup. He moved to Chelsea for around £20 million in the January 2011 transfer window and became a cult hero overnight for his man-of-the-match performances against Fulham, Manchester City and Napoli in the Champions League. Chelsea somehow overcame Barcelona in the semi-final but weren't expected to beat Bayern Munich at the Allianz Arena. A late Didier Drogba header took the match to extra time but it would eventually go to penalties. Luiz converted his but Oli and Schweinsteiger missed for Bayern and Chelsea won the trophy for the first time.

His excellent domestic performances with both Benfica and Chelsea attracted the attention of Mano Menezes and he made his international debut in a 2-0 win against the United States in late 2010. He was also called up for the 2011 Copa América but injury prevented him from starting. He was back to full fitness the following season and captained Brazil for their 1-0 win over South Africa. In early 2013 he played alongside Chelsea team-mate Oscar against Russia at Stamford Bridge.

If Luiz can stay fit and continue to deliver solid defensive performances for Chelsea and Brazil, he will definitely feature at the 2014 World Cup in his home country.

Name: David Luiz (Moreira Marinho)
Born: April 22nd 1987, Diadema
Position: Defender
International Career: 2010 -
Caps: 20
Goals: 0
Honours: Copa América Squad (2011)

Luisão

Luisão began his professional career with local side Atlético Juventus in 1999 but he transferred to Cruzeiro the following year and his knack of scoring important goals brought him to the attention of the national selectors. He made his debut in 2001 but couldn't force his way into Luiz Felipe Scolari's World Cup squad in 2002, although by the 2004 Copa América he was captain. He played in all six matches and scored his first international goal in the final as Brazil overcame Argentina.

He was in the squad for the 2006 World Cup defence but didn't play in any of the matches, although when Dunga took over as coach after the unsuccessful tournament he was back in favour. He played four matches during the 2009 Confederations Cup campaign, including the final, a 3-2 win over the United States, and earned selection to the 2010 World Cup in South Africa on the back of good club performances for Benfica, who he had joined in 2003. He'd helped the Portuguese side to the league title in 2005 and played 45

Above: *Luisão*

games in a successful 2009/10 season in which Benfica won the league, Portuguese Cup and reached the last eight of the Europa League. The World Cup was a disappointment for Brazil, however, and they lost in the quarter-final.

Luisão was then involved in a bizarre incident in which he collided with referee Christian Fischer as the official was about to send off team-mate Javi Garcia. The referee suspended the match and took legal action against Luisão, with the Brazilian being banned for two months and heavily fined. He made his last appearance for the national team in 2011 but is still a regular starter with Benfica.

Name: Luisão (Ânderson Luís da Silva)
Born: February 13th 1981, Amparo
Position: Defender
International Career: 2001 - 2011
Caps: 43
Goals: 3
Honours: Copa América (2004), Confederations Cup (2005, 2009)

Maicon

Right: *Brazil's forward Nilmar (left) celebrates his third goal against Chile with teammate Maicon*

Maicon played for Grêmio's youth team before joining Cruzeiro in 2001. He enjoyed three years with the club before moving to European side Monaco. In three seasons he made 59 league appearances and scored five goals from right back and it was only a matter of time before one of the European powerhouses secured his signature. He eventually chose to join Internazionale in Milan.

He was solid defensively but was better known for his blistering runs down the flanks, pinpoint crossing and fierce right-footed shot. During a Champions League game against Valencia in 2007 he was embroiled in an altercation with David Navarro and was banned for three matches but he returned to help Inter win their fourth consecutive league title and scored a match-winning brace against Siena.

The 2009/10 season was even more successful and Maicon's trademark runs and vital goals saw Inter win the Scudetto, the Coppa Italia (against Roma) and the Champions League final (against Bayern Munich in the Santiago Bernabéu in Madrid). He was promptly named defender of

the year by UEFA and also received a nomination for the Ballon d'Or as the finest player in Europe. His next domestic season was quiet and he signed for Manchester City for the 2012/13 campaign.

He was first called up by Brazil in 2003 but he didn't make the World Cup squad until the 2010 tournament in South Africa. He scored the first goal in Brazil's 2-1 win over North Korea and managed to keep Didier Drogba and Cristiano Ronaldo quiet for most of their second and third matches against the Ivory Coast and Portugal respectively. Maicon started the knockout game against Chile, which ended up as an easy 3-0 win, but they were then beaten by the brutal but brilliant Dutch in the quarter-final. It remains to be seen if his club performances with Manchester City earn this devastating wing-back a recall to the international side in time for the 2014 World Cup in his home country.

Name: Maicon (Douglas Sisenando)
Born: July 26th 1981, Novo Hamburgo
Position: Right back
International Career: 2003 - 2011
Caps: 66
Goals: 6
Honours: Copa América (2004, 2007), Confederations Cup (2005, 2009), World Cup Squad (2010)

Marcelo

Right: *Marcelo*

Marcelo came from a very poor background in the favelas but he was supremely talented and soon attracted the attention of Fluminese. He stayed with the club for three years as a youth and two seasons as a professional before he was snapped up by Real Madrid in 2007. With his pace, vision and lethal shot, he was immediately hailed as Roberto Carlos's successor. But new coach Juande Ramos opted for a more defensive approach after a poor run of results and started with Gabriel Heinze instead. Marcelo was then switched to the left wing but when José Mourinho became manager of Real in 2010 he moved Marcelo back to his preferred position. His superb form led to praise from Diego Maradona who called him the third best player in La Liga after Lionel Messi and Cristiano Ronaldo.

Marcelo made his international debut against Wales at White Hart Lane and scored a goal in his side's 2-0 victory. Dunga used him at the 2008 Beijing Olympics and the side collected the bronze medal, but he was not picked for the full squad at the 2010 World Cup in South Africa and Brazil performed poorly. Marcelo was back in favour when new coach Mano Menezes took the reins after the World Cup and he is now the first-choice left back for both club and country.

His overlapping runs, deadly crosses and fierce finishing make him one of the most feared left backs in world football. At only 25, he is sure to be on the scene for many more years and, barring injury, will certainly feature at the 2014 World Cup.

Name: Marcelo (Vieira da Silva Júnior)
Born: May 12th 1988, Rio de Janeiro
Position: Left back
International Career: 2006 –
Caps: 18
Goals: 4
Honours: Olympic Bronze Medal (2008), Olympic Silver Medal (2012)

Mazzola

Mazzola began his professional career with Palmeiras in 1956. He was a prolific goal-scorer (34 in 62 league matches in only two seasons) who only came to worldwide attention when he signed for Milan in 1958. In seven years with the club he scored 120 goals in 205 games. He then transferred to Napoli and scored another 71 goals in 180 league starts. He spent the last four years of his domestic career with Juventus and became the joint fourth highest scorer in Serie A history. He also holds the record (with Lionel Messi) of scoring the most European Cup (now Champions League) goals in one season with 14.

He was called up to the Brazilian national team for the World Cup qualifying campaign in 1957. He promptly scored Brazil's first goal of the tournament proper against Austria in a comfortable 3-0 win (he also scored the third). He played against England in their second match (the first goal-less game in World Cup history) but was dropped in favour of Pelé for the final group match against the Soviet Union. He was back in the starting line-up against Wales but had to settle for a place on the bench for the 5-2 demolition of France in the semi-final and for the final against Sweden (which Brazil won by the same score).

This marked the end of his career with Brazil but he qualified to play for Italy having lived in the country for 18 years and he scored five goals in six appearances for his adopted nation in the build-up to the 1962 World Cup in Chile.

Above: *President Lula presents Mazzola with his old jersey*

> **Name:** Mazzola (José João Altafini)
> **Born:** August 24th 1938, Piracicaba
> **Position:** Striker
> **International Career:** 1957 – 1962
> **Caps:** 14
> **Goals:** 9
> **Honours:** World Cup Winner (1958)

Müller

Müller began his senior career with São Paulo in 1984. He was a deadly finisher and scored 25 goals in 60 games in his first three years. He never really settled at any particular club, however, and over the next 20 years he played for Torino, São Paulo, Kashiwa Reysol, Palmeiras, Perugia, Santos, Cruzeiro and Corinthians (amongst others). He scored roughly a goal every three games and was called up to the national squad for the 1986 World Cup in Mexico. He only played a supporting role, which he reprised in Italy four years later.

He came on against Cameroon in the World Cup in the USA in 1994 but was an unused sub against the hosts in the first knockout game as well as in the quarter-final against the Netherlands in Dallas. He also had to make do with a place on the bench in the semi-final against Sweden and the final against Italy.

In all he scored 12 goals for Brazil in 56 games but he retired when he realised he wasn't going to make the final squad for the 1998 World Cup in France. He hung up his boots for good in 2004 to concentrate on a TV career.

Name: Müller (Luís Antônio Corrêa da Costa)
Born: January 31st 1966, Campo Grande
Position: Striker
International Career: 1986 – 1998
Caps: 56
Goals: 12
Honours: World Cup Winner (1994)

Neymar

Neymar is already drawing comparisons with Argentine superstar Lionel Messi and he looks set to dominate planet football for the next decade. He had a long and distinguished youth career from the age of seven with Portuguesa Santista and then Santos, and he signed for the latter to begin his professional career in 2009. In his first 100 league matches he demonstrated his exceptional skill, devastating pace and silky dribbling, and his 56 goals saw him immediately drafted into the national squad.

In 2010 he helped Santos to the Campeonato Paulista (league) and Copa do Brasil double and was voted the club's best player for the next two seasons. Pelé and Romário urged Dunga to select him for the 2010 World Cup in South Africa but Dunga omitted him because he was too inexperienced and hadn't yet made the transition from talented club player to top international. Dunga left after the disappointing tournament and new coach Mano Menezes recalled Neymar for matches against the USA and Scotland. He scored three goals in the two matches and then helped Brazil to the quarter-final of the Copa América.

Along with Oscar, Sandro and Alexandre Pato – all of whom starred at the London 2012 Olympics – he looks likely to lift Brazilian football to the heights it enjoyed in the glory years of the early 1970s and 1980s. Barring injury, he will almost certainly feature at the 2014 World Cup on home soil.

Above: Neymar playing against Scotland in 2011

Name: Neymar (da Silva Santos Júnior)
Born: February 5th 1992, Mogi das Cruzes
Position: Striker
International Career: 2010 –
Caps: 32
Goals: 20
Honours: Superclásico de las Américas (2011, 2012), Olympic Silver Medal (2012)

Oscar, José

Oscar began his career with local side Ponte Preta in 1972 but he had seven quiet seasons with the club before spending a year with New York Cosmos. In 1980 he joined São Paulo where he remained for seven years and 294 appearances. He was first called up to the national team in 1978 but, despite Brazil not losing a game at that year's World Cup in Argentina, Brazil were eliminated on goal difference after the hosts thrashed Peri in suspicious circumstances.

He was again solid in defence at the 1982 World Cup in Spain, with Brazil winning all three of their group matches and only conceding two goals. Although they then beat Argentina in the second group phase, a memorable Paolo Rossi hat-trick knocked them out of the competition. Oscar was in the squad in the lead-up to the 1986 World Cup in Mexico but he didn't play any matches in the tournament and wasn't picked again.

He played on for three more years before moving into management with a number of clubs in Japan and Brazil.

Name: Oscar (José Oscar Bernardi)
Born: June 20th 1954, Monte Siao
Position: Defender
International Career: 1978 – 1986
Caps: 60
Goals: 2
Honours: World Cup Squad (1978, 1982, 1986)

Oscar, dos Santos

Oscar is another supremely gifted midfield maestro who came through the youth system at União Barbarense before joining São Paulo, but a contractual dispute then led to his departure. In 2010 he signed for Internacional but he only stayed for two seasons, during which he started 36 league matches and scored 11 goals. He then moved to Europe to join Chelsea for around £20 million. He soon established a good relationship with Eden Hazard and Juan Mata and helped the side to the knockout stages of the Champions League.

He was drafted into the national team for the London Olympics, and every goal Brazil scored was either put away or assisted by Oscar and Neymar. They lost to Mexico in the final but he then made his full debut against Argentina. In 2012 he scored against their archrivals in a friendly, although Brazil lost 4-3. His skilful dribbling, incisive runs and great vision make him an asset to any team and he's sure to add to his 15 international caps in the build-up to the 2014 World Cup.

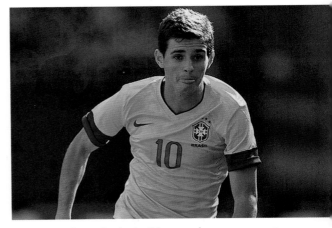

Above: *Oscar dos Santos Emboaba Júnior*

Name: Oscar (dos Santos Emboaba Júnior)
Born: September 9th 1991, Américana
Position: Attacking midfield
International Career: 2011 –
Caps: 15
Goals: 5
Honours: Superclásico de las Américas (2011), Olympic Silver Medal (2012)

Pato

Alexandre Pato enjoyed six years with the Internacional youth team. He graduated to the senior side in 2006 and scored 12 league goals in his first season. Italian giants Milan lured him to Europe the following year and he made an immediate but lasting impression, scoring 51 goals in 117 league appearances during six years with the club.

He was called up by Brazil in the lead-up to the 2008 Summer Olympics and scored on his debut against Sweden at Arsenal's Emirates Stadium, but Dunga controversially left him out of the 2010 World Cup squad. The tournament was a disappointment and Dunga was replaced by Mano Menezes who recalled Pato. He continued to score vital goals and was again picked for the Olympics in 2012. Menezes used him twice early in 2013 and he should make the World Cup squad for Brazil 2014.

Name: Alexandre Pato (Rodrigues da Silva)
Born: September 2nd 1989, Pato Branco
Position: Striker
International Career: 2008 –
Caps: 24
Goals: 9
Honours: Confederations Cup (2009)

Paulinho

Paulinho started his youth career with Pão de Açúar but then surprisingly transferred to FC Vilnius in Latvia in 2006. Having then moved to Poland for a season, he signed for Bragantino and soon attracted the interest of Corinthians. He signed for the Brazilian giants in 2010 and in his first 85 league games he scored 19 goals. In 2012 he helped the side to the Club World Cup and was immediately targeted by several European giants. He made his international debut in 2011 and his powerful runs, box-to-box stamina and solid defence should see him selected for Brazil at the 2014 World Cup.

Name: Paulinho (José Paulo Bezerra Maciel Júnior)
Born: July 25th 1988, São Paulo
Position: Midfielder
International Career: 2011 -
Caps: 11
Goals: 2
Honours: Superclásico de las Américas (2011, 2012)

Pelé

Pelé is the embodiment of Brazilian football, playing the game to a samba beat with spellbinding flair and creativity. His autobiography coined the phrase the Beautiful Game and there can be no more fitting description of his own ability. Pelé played as an inside forward, striker and playmaker with visionary passing, slalom-like dribbling, and an almost supernatural goal-scoring ability. With over a thousand goals, he also holds the record for being the youngest winner of the World Cup and is the only player to have won the World Cup three times. After collecting his third winners' medal, the headline in the English newspaper, *The Times*, read: "How do you spell Pelé? G-O-D."

Pelé was born in Minais Gerais, a state in the southeast of Brazil. He had a fairly typical Brazilian upbringing, living in a small and crowded house with a leaking roof. His family struggled to make ends meet but he ended up playing football in the streets with his friends. Unable to afford a real football, they would play with a sock stuffed with newspapers and rags and tied up with string. Despite material hardship, it was a close family and his parents taught him to respect the innate qualities of people, the importance of keeping a promise, and to live with dignity. It was these personal qualities that people around the world would come to love later in his life, as much as the sublime football he played.

Still a child, his family moved to Baurú in the interior of São Paulo state. His father, Dondinho, was also a professional player. The family moved with him but a serious knee injury ended his career prematurely. Dondinho became the young Edson's first coach and biggest fan. Originally nicknamed Dico by the family (he ended up fighting with schoolmates who started calling him Pelé), his prodigious talent shone through. Having stood by his father, his mother worried about the insecurity of a footballer's life and wanted something better for her son. Pelé wanted to help supplement his family's income so he began shining shoes but he made little money and convinced his mother to allow him to work at the Baurú Athletic Club stadium on match days and at

the railway stations in town. It was around this time that his aunt Maria gave him his first pairs of shoes, which had belonged to her boss's son. He was only allowed to wear them for church and special occasions but he soon ruined them when he decided to see what it was like to play football in shoes rather than barefoot.

At the age of 11 he was playing for an amateur team called Ameriquinha when his flair was spotted by former World Cup player Waldemar de Brito. De Brito asked him to join the youth team he coached and, when he reached 15, Waldemar took him for a trial at Santos football club in São Paulo. Waldemar declared to a disbelieving board that Pelé would become the greatest soccer player in the world. Pelé soon made his senior team debut, scoring as a substitute in September 1956 when he was still only 15. In the first league game he played for Santos he scored four goals. The next season he established himself in the first team and finished as São Paulo state's top scorer with 32 goals.

Pelé's meteoric rise continued and he was called up in 1957 to make his international debut against Argentina, scoring the only goal in a 2-1 loss. However, at the 1958 World Cup in Sweden, the virtually unknown 17-year-old thrilled the world and became an instant legend. After Brazil's two opening group games, Pelé made his World Cup entrance against the USSR. Although he did not score, Brazil won 2-0. In the quarter-final Pelé scored the only goal to knock Wales out, before scoring a hat-trick in a 5-2 demolition of France to put Brazil into the final. The final was a classic demonstration of attacking football and flair with Brazil hammering hosts Sweden 5-2 to win the World Cup for the first time. Pelé scored twice: the first included controlling the ball on his chest, flicking a beautiful but

Above: *Pelé in training for Brazil's match against England*

precise lob over the nearest defender, before quickly nipping around him to volley into the net. Pelé, the youngest winner of the World Cup, crying tears of joy while being hugged by his team-mates after the final whistle, will remain an iconic image of the world's greatest competition.

Pelé continued his phenomenal form with Santos, where he remained top scorer for every season between 1957 and 1965 – during which Santos dominated the Campeonato Paulista (state league championship) in 1958, 1960, 1961, 1962, 1964, 1965, 1967, 1968, 1969 and 1973, the national Taça Brasil in 1961, 1962, 1963, 1964 and 1965, as well as the Copa Libertadores (beating Peñaro of Uruguay 3-0 in a replay in 1962, and Boca Juniors of

Argentina 5-3 on aggregate in 1963). Santos soon capitalised on the Black Pearl's fame and travelled the world to play exhibition matches against its top teams (Pelé received a percentage from each game and became one of the era's best-paid athletes). By the 1962 World Cup finals in Chile, Pelé was a global sensation. Brazil started with a 2-0 victory over Mexico with Pelé scoring a wonder goal after dribbling past four players before beating the keeper. However, ten minutes into the next match against Czechoslovakia he pulled a thigh muscle trying a long-range shot and did not play again. Brazil won the trophy by beating Czechoslovakia 3-1 when they faced each other again in the final itself.

With the elite European clubs trying to sign him, it is rumoured that the government of Brazil declared Pelé an official national treasure to prevent him moving overseas. If 1962 had been a disappointment, 1966 was even worse as Brazil struggled in England. They lost against Hungary 3-1 (during which Pelé was rested), before playing against a violent Portuguese side. They literally kicked him out of the tournament, much to the disgust of spectators and commentators, and Brazil were knocked out at the first group stage. Pelé immediately announced that he would not play again in the World Cup after such bad treatment and a lack of protection from the referees.

In 1967, his appearance with Santos during a short tour of exhibition matches in Nigeria resulted in a 48-hour ceasefire in the Biafran Civil War so that both sides could watch him play. Pelé hit another incredible milestone by scoring his thousandth goal, a penalty, against Vasco da Gama in 1969. Known as O Milésimo (The Thousandth), it was widely celebrated in Brazil, and he dedicated it to all the poor children in the country.

Luckily for Brazil and the football world, Pelé was persuaded to return for his final World Cup in Mexico in 1970. Playing alongside Jairzinho, Rivelino, Carlos Alberto, Gérson, and Tostão, he was sensational and many believe they formed the nucleus of the best team ever seen on a football pitch. They were drawn in a tough group that included Czechoslovakia, Romania and defending world champions England. Brazil beat Czechoslovakia 4-1, with Pelé scoring one and narrowly missing an audacious chip over Czech goalkeeper Ivo Viktor from the halfway line. In an unforgettable and high-quality match, England, who defended brilliantly, were beaten 1-0 by a Jairzinho goal (set up by Pelé). Earlier, he'd seemed certain to score with a bullet header but Gordon Banks somehow denied him with a flying dive to scoop the ball away before it crossed the line. It is commonly referred to as the "Save of the Century" and Pelé called it the best save he had ever seen. He opened the scoring against Romania from a free-kick and then added a second before the game ended 3-2. In the quarter-final Brazil beat Peru 4-2, before they defeated Uruguay 3-1 in the semi-final. The game also contained another piece of Pelé brilliance as he broke free of the defence to chase a ball knocked into space by Tostão. Uruguayan keeper Ladislao Mazurkiewicz raced off his line to meet the ball, but Pelé sent the ball right as he ran left, leaving the keeper in no-man's land. Pelé then turned and shot but he dragged the ball narrowly wide. Brazil outplayed Italy in the final, running out 4-1 winners. Pelé scored a header and claimed two assists and Brazil were crowned champions for an unprecedented third time. They were allowed to keep the Jules Rimet trophy permanently.

Pelé wanted to leave the game while he was still at the top so he played his last international match in a 2-2 draw against Yugoslavia in 1971. He stayed with Santos for four more successful years, eventually retiring in 1974, after which Santos retired his number ten jersey in tribute. However, he was soon tempted out of retirement to play in the lucrative North American Soccer

Above: *Brazil's Pelé (left) celebrates*

League (NASL) for the New York Cosmos in a multi-million-dollar deal (rumoured to be worth between $2.8 million and $4.5 million). Despite being past his prime, he still sparkled and brought a level of glamour to the NASL before he retired for good in 1977. His last game was an emotional exhibition match against Santos. He played one half for each team before being carried on his colleagues' shoulders around the Giants' stadium in front of a capacity crowd.

After such an illustrious career, Pelé devoted much of his time to charities helping underprivileged children through the United Nations Children Fund (UNICEF), as well as being made Brazil's Minister of Sport for three years. As well as advertising sponsorship, he has written an autobiography, and appeared in a number of films and documentaries, including starring alongside Michael Caine and Sylvester Stallone in the 1981 classic *Escape to Victory*. He is still an influential presence on football's global stage and is revered around the world for his skill, his passion for the beautiful game, his sportsmanship and his humility.

> **Name:** Pelé (Edson Arantes do Nascimento)
> **Born:** October 23rd 1940, Três Corações
> **Position:** Striker
> **International Career:** 1957 – 1971
> **Caps:** 92
> **Goals:** 77
> **Honours:** World Cup Winner (1958, 1962, 1970)

Pepe

Pepe was another one-club man who developed into one of the most feared and potent wings / strikers in the game. He spent his entire professional career (1954-1969) with Santos and eventually made 750 league appearances and scored 405 goals. His astonishing ability on the ball and deadly finishing saw him drafted into the national team before the 1958 World Cup but he wasn't good enough to oust Garrincha or Pelé from the team and could only warm the bench for the victorious campaign. He suffered on the subs' bench again four years later when Brazil defended the title in Chile but his form between the tournaments saw him net 22 times in only 41 internationals.

He retired in 1969 but returned four years later to manage his beloved Santos to victory in the Campeonato Paulista (top-flight state championship). Over the next 30 years he would coach another nine teams, most notably Peru in 1989. In 2004/05 he took charge of Al-Ahli with Pep Guardiola as his understudy.

Above: *Pepe today*

Name: Pepe (José Macia)
Born: February 25th 1935, Santos
Position: Wing
International Career: 1955 – 1965
Caps: 41
Goals: 22
Honours: World Cup Squad (1958, 1962)

Pereira

Luís Pereira began his career at São Bento in 1967 but he didn't make an impact on the national sport until he joined Palmeiras the following year. He played 562 games for the club and also racked up 171 appearances for Atlético Madrid after moving to Europe in 1974.

The national team was struggling in the early 1970s after the departure of Pelé and several of the stars of the 1970 World Cup so Luís Pereira was drafted in to bring some stability to the defensive line. He won the first of his 38 caps in 1973 but was sent off at the following year's World Cup in Germany after a foul on Johan Neeskens. Neeskens and Cruyff then scored to eliminate the holders. He wasn't selected for the 1978 World Cup in Argentina but continued playing at domestic level until 1994.

Name: Luís (Edmundo) Pereira
Born: June 21st 1949, Juazeiro
Position: Defender
International Career: 1973 – 1977
Caps: 38
Goals: 1
Honours: World Cup Squad (1974)

Peres

Waldir Peres started his career with local sides Garça and Ponte Preta before signing for São Paulo in 1973. He was tipped for greatness and was first capped by the national side the following year. He was also selected for the 1974 World Cup in Germany, but he didn't make the starting line-up and Brazil were eventually beaten by the Dutch masters of total football. They then lost the third-place match to Poland. Four years later they were arguably the victims of a fixed match when hosts Argentina thrashed neighbours Peru 6-0, the goal difference dumping Brazil out of the tournament despite them not losing a match.

In 1982, Brazil were back to their best and were expected to win the World Cup in Spain. Their established stars like Sócrates, Falcão and Zico saw them breeze past the Soviet Union, Scotland and New Zealand, and they then overcame Argentina 3-1 to set up a meeting with Italy. The contest was expected to pitch the brilliant Brazilian attack against the tight Italian defence but Paolo Rossi struck

Above: *Waldir Peres with the squad at the 1982 World Cup*

a stunning hat-trick past Waldir Peres and Brazil were eliminated. This proved to be the goalkeeper's international swansong as he was not picked again by his country. He played on with a variety of domestic clubs until 1990, however.

Name: Waldir Peres (de Arruda)
Born: January 2nd 1951, Garça
Position: Goalkeeper
International Career: 1975 - 1982
Caps: 30
Goals: 0
Honours: World Cup Squad (1974, 1978, 1982)

Piazza

Wilson Piazza only played for three teams in a career spanning nearly 20 years: domestic outfits Renasença (1961-1964) and Cruzeiro FC (1964-1979); and the national team from 1969-1975. He was a solid central defender or defensive midfielder who forced his way into the Brazil team just in time for the 1970 World Cup in Mexico. He played in every game and in the final he lined up alongside Brito, Carlos Alberto and Everaldo. The quartet denied Italy so much time and space that they could only manage a single goal. When you've the likes of Jairzinho, Gérson, Tostão, Rivelino and Pelé going forward, goals aren't going to be a problem and Brazil duly won the match 4-1.

He played in the group stage of the 1974 World Cup but was then relegated to the substitutes' bench for crucial matches against East Germany, Argentina and the Netherlands. Brazil won the first two but looked creaky defensively against the Dutch and were eliminated by goals from Neeskens and Cruyff in a bad-tempered match. He retired from international football the following year with 47 caps under his belt, and he played on with Cruzeiro until 1979.

Name: Wilson (da Silva) Piazza
Born: February 25th 1943, Ribeirão das Neves
Position: Defender
International Career: 1969 - 1975
Caps: 47
Goals: 0
Honours: World Cup Winner (1970)

Ramires

Ramires's youth career began with Royal Sport Club in 2004 but he then graduated to the professional ranks with Cruzeiro having also played for Joinville. In the next two years he scored 10 goals in 61 league appearances, but he then signed for Benfica for a single glorious season in which they won the league and the Portuguese Cup. Chelsea came calling in 2010 and he signed for the London club for around £20 million. He had a solid first season but 2012 would see his career take off: he helped Chelsea to the FA Cup and then scored the goal that knocked out Barcelona and took the club to the Champions League final, despite the fact that accumulated bookings kept him out of the match against Bayern Munich.

He was first called up by Brazil in place of Robinho at the 2008 Olympics in Beijing. He played four matches and helped the side to the bronze medal. He then became a regular in the side during the 2009 Confederations Cup and for the qualifying tournament for the 2010 World Cup. He picked up a suspension in South Africa, however, which many, including coach Dunga, believe cost them the quarter-final against the Dutch.

He is surprisingly quick, possesses two good feet and excellent stamina. If he can stay fit, he should make the 2014 World Cup squad for his home tournament.

Name: Ramires (Santos do Nascimento)
Born: March 24th 1987, Barra do Piraí
Position: Midfield
International Career: 2009 –
Caps: 34
Goals: 3
Honours: Olympic Bronze Medal (2008), Confederations Cup (2009)

Ramos

Mauro Ramos was a solid defender who played for the Sanjoanense youth team before graduating to São Paulo FC in 1948 – where he remained for 11 years – and then Santos to see out his career. He was called up to the national team in 1949 but, despite helping them to the Copa América, he wasn't selected for the 1950 World Cup and didn't play a match during the 1954 tournament.

He was sidelined again for the 1958 World Cup in Sweden and only made his tournament debut four years later in Chile. It was worth the wait, however. As captain of the 1962 side, he led them to the title with victory over Czechoslovakia in the final. He played on for the national team until 1965 and finally retired in 1968 after a brief spell in Mexico with Deportivo Toluca.

Name: Mauro Ramos (de Oliveira)
Born: August 30th 1930, Poços de Caldas
Died: September 18th 2002
Position: Defender
International Career: 1949 – 1965
Caps: 30
Goals: 0
Honours: World Cup Squad (1954, 1958), World Cup Winner (1962)

Rildo

Rildo began his club career with local side Recife but he was snapped up by Botafogo within a year. During his time with them he was drafted into a national team that had won two World Cups on the trot and featured some of the greatest players in the history of the game: Pelé, Garrincha, Vavá and Didi. However, at the next tournament in England these marvellous players were targeted by the likes of Hungary and Portugal and they were effectively kicked out of the event. (He scored his only international goal in the 3-1 defeat to the Portuguese.) Despite the disappointment, they were determined to rebuild in time for the 1970 World Cup in Mexico.

Rildo was an integral cog in the defensive line throughout the qualifying campaign. He'd recently transferred to Santos and his form alongside the other Golden Era players like Pepe, Coutinho and Clodoaldo was sensational. He captained the side to three state championships (1967, 1968 and 1969) but

Left: *Rildo evades a sliding tackle*

was then inexplicably left out of the squad for the World Cup and he could only watch as the greatest team in history swept all before them and lifted the trophy.

Rildo's career then declined and he ended up joining Pelé at New York Cosmos in 1977. He remained in the United States until hanging up his boots in 1980. Ten years later he moved into management with the California Emperors. He is now in the UK with Marlborough School.

Name: Rildo (da Costa Menezes)
Born: January 23rd 1942, Recife
Position: Defender
International Career: 1963 - 1969
Caps: 38
Goals: 1
Honours: World Cup Squad (1966)

Rivaldo

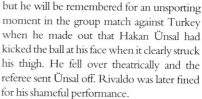

Rivaldo began his career with Santa Cruz and over the next two decades he would develop into one of the most influential and deadly playmakers and goal-scorers in the game. He had brief spells with Mogi Mirim, Corinthians and Palmeiras before he arrived in Europe with Deportivo La Coruña. He scored 21 goals in his first 41 league matches and attracted the attention of Barcelona. He joined the Catalans in 1997, helped them to the league and cup double in his first season and scored another 86 league goals in 157 appearances. In 1999 he won another league title and was voted World Player of the Year.

He made his debut in the yellow of Brazil in 1993 and scored the only goal in a friendly against Mexico. He was blamed for their defeat at the 1996 Olympics to Nigeria, however, and coach Mário Zagallo dropped him until 1998 when he earned a recall for the World Cup in France. He helped the team reach the final but they were poor against the hosts and lost 3-0. Rivaldo made amends at the next tournament in the Far East. He scored goals in each of their first five matches and then set up Ronaldo twice in the final against Germany,

but he will be remembered for an unsporting moment in the group match against Turkey when he made out that Hakan Ünsal had kicked the ball at his face when it clearly struck his thigh. He fell over theatrically and the referee sent Ünsal off. Rivaldo was later fined for his shameful performance.

He made his last appearance for the national team in 2003, although he carried on at club level with Olympiacos and AEK Athens amongst others. Despite his occasional falling out with coaches or bad sportsmanship, Rivaldo was one of the most technically gifted players of his generation. He was strong with both feet, had a surge of pace and could hold off defenders to slide crucial passes to the likes of Romário and Ronaldo.

Name: Rivaldo (Vítor Borba Ferreira)
Born: April 19th 1972, Paulista
Position: Attacking midfield
International Career: 1993 – 2003
Caps: 74
Goals: 34
Honours: Confederations Cup (1997), Copa América (1999), World Cup Winner (2002)

Rivelino

Rivelino's career began at Barcelona in 1962 but he then signed for youth side Corinthians in 1963. Two years later he graduated to the senior team and he quickly developed into one of the finest midfielders in the game. With his raking long passes, thunderbolt free-kicks and silky touch, he became a fan favourite and he eventually made 471 league appearances for Corinthians. In those nine years he also scored 141 goals, but he then signed for Fluminese, where his record, if anything, improved slightly: 53 goals in 158 league starts and two championships (1975 and 1976).

A player of Rivelino's class couldn't be ignored by the national selectors and he made the first of his 92 starts for Brazil in 1965. He didn't play any part in the disastrous World Cup campaign in England the following year but he was an integral part of the all-conquering 1970 World Cup team. He scored three goals in the tournament, including a wonder free-kick against Czechoslovakia. He had less success in 1974 and 1978 in a side that clearly missed the genius of Pelé and the flair of Tostão, Gérson and Jairzinho.

He retired from international football after the World Cup in Argentina but continued his domestic career with Al-Hilal in Saudi Arabia. He hung up his boots for good in 1981 but as a player he will always be mentioned in the same breath as Zico, Sócrates and the greatest of them all, Pelé.

Name: Roberto Rivelino
Born: January 1st 1946, São Paulo
Position: Attacking midfield
International Career: 1965 – 1978
Caps: 92
Goals: 26
Honours: World Cup Winner (1970)

Robinho

Below: *Robinho takes on the Swiss defence*

When he saw a 15-year-old Robinho play, Pelé believed he had seen his rightful heir. He joined Santos in 2002 and, in four seasons with the club, played 147 league matches and scored 61 goals. Several European giants arrived with their chequebooks open but Santos refused to sell Robinho until after he'd recovered from his mother's kidnap ordeal. He finally moved to Real Madrid for £20 million in 2005 and he scored 25 league goals in 101 appearances during two title-winning seasons.

When Robinho found out he was going to be moved on in favour of Cristiano Ronaldo, he said he would only transfer to Chelsea, but he eventually signed for Manchester City for £32 million after the club was bought out by the Abu Dhabi United Group. He had a solid first season but an injury meant he only played 12 matches in 2009/10 and he then returned to Santos on loan. Later that year he joined Milan and immediately helped himself to the Scudetto.

He made his debut in the yellow of Brazil at the 2003 CONCACAF Gold Cup match against Mexico. He put the disappointment of the loss behind him and helped the team win the 2005 Confederations Cup and the 2007 Copa América. He was the tournament's best player in the latter, and his goals then helped Brazil win the 2009 Confederations Cup. Brazil were expected to shine at the World Cup the following year but only Robinho seemed to have the appetite for success. He scored in their game against Chile and backed it up with another against the Netherlands, although the Dutch scored again and eliminated Brazil, 2-1.

Name: Robinho (Robson de Souza)
Born: January 25th 1984, São Vicente
Position: Wing
International Career: 2003 –
Caps: 90
Goals: 26
Honours: Confederations Cup (2005, 2009), Copa América (2007)

Romário

Above: *Romário with the World Cup*

Romário began his youth career with Olaria and then Vasco da Gama, and he graduated to the latter's senior side in 1985. He wasn't a prolific goal-scorer in his first three years but a move to PSV Eindhoven saw him explode onto the world stage with 96 league goals in only 107 games in his first five seasons. He then signed for Barcelona, Flamengo and Valencia, but the goals kept coming and in his league career he would eventually score 309 in 448 games. Overall, he would become one of the only players in history to score more than 1,000 goals, although this did include 77 scored in friendlies and youth games.

He was voted World Player of the Year in 1994 after teaming up with strike partner Bebeto during the glorious World Cup campaign in the USA. In his later years he played alongside Ronaldo and the pair each bagged a hat-trick in the final of the 1997 Confederations Cup against Australia. He was controversially left out of the squad for the 1998 World Cup in France but he later admitted to having a muscle injury, and he was overlooked again four years later by Luiz Felipe Scolari on the grounds of indiscipline. He played his last game in the yellow of Brazil in a tribute match against Guatemala in 2005.

There can be no doubt that Romário was one of the best striker's in the game's history. His turn of pace, devastating swerve and clinical and ruthless finishing would have allowed him to play at the highest level in any era. His overall record for his country (which includes matches played at the Olympics) is bettered only by Pelé.

Name: Romário (de Souza Faria)
Born: January 29th 1966, Rio de Janeiro
Position: Striker
International Career: 1987 – 2005
Caps: 85
Goals: 71
Honours: Copa América (1989, 1997), World Cup Winner (1994), Confederations Cup (1997)

Ronaldinho

Ronaldinho blushes when he is compared with Pelé and Zico, and, when asked by a journalist how he felt about being the best player in the world, he simply answered that he did not feel he was the best player at Barcelona. However, such modesty cannot hide his irrepressible skills and achievements: FIFA World Player of the Year in 2004 and 2005, as well as European Player of the Year in 2005. His best position is just behind the strikers but his technical ability and flair mean he can operate anywhere in attack or midfield. In Brazil he is commonly referred to as Ronaldinho Gaúcho to distinguish himself from his namesake Ronaldo (who is already referred to as Ronaldinho or "little Ronaldo"). Gaúcho is the name commonly used for people from the Rio Grande do Sul region of Brazil.

Ronaldo Assis de Moreira was born in a favela in Porto Alegre, Brazil on 21st March 1980. His father was a shipyard worker and stadium security guard, while his mother worked as a civil servant at the town hall. When his older brother, Roberto, started playing professionally for one of the city's major teams, Grêmio, it provided the family with financial security. In an attempt to convince the young star not to move to Europe, the club bought the family a nice villa to live in. It was here, tragically, that his father, João, died in an accident in the family pool when Ronaldinho was eight, so Roberto began looking after his family. His own career, however, was cut short by injury before he could reach his potential.

Before soccer, Ronaldinho loved playing futsal (a form of fast indoor five-a-side soccer) and beach football, which, in part, explains some of his exceptional close control. The youngster's prodigious talent was recognised early, with his brother taking him to Grêmio's youth set-up. He was even captured on film scoring twenty-three goals in a 23-0 win. Recognition followed as he starred in Brazil's Under-17 World Cup win in Egypt, where he was named as the best player in the tournament. In 1998 he made his professional debut for Grêmio and a year later he debuted for Brazil's senior team against Latvia. He then came on as a substitute in the Copa América to score an exceptional goal in a 7–0 demolition of Venezuela. Later that year he was part of the Brazilian squad in the Confederations Cup. He scored in every game he played but was injured for the final, which they lost 4–3 to Mexico. With his club, he scored 22 goals and helped Grêmio win the Campeonato Gaúcho (state championship) and the Copa Sul (the regional Southern Cup) in 1999. However, in 2000, his contract expired. Despite being happy at the club, he looked for a new challenge. With Europe beckoning, top French side Paris Saint-Germain (PSG) underwent months of intense negotiations before Ronaldinho was finally allowed to leave for the bargain price of 4.5 million euros in 2001.

Ronaldinho's skills continued to develop during his two seasons at PSG but he also hit the headlines over his disciplinary problems and his partying on the Parisian nightclub scene. Even so, he still scored 68 goals and played a significant part in Brazil's 2002 World Cup victory in South Korea – including scoring the winner against England in the quarter-final with an audacious free kick before being sent off seven minutes later. Another season and more controversy followed at PSG, when he stated publicly that he wanted to move on. The elite clubs lined up for his signature and for a long time it looked like he would become a Manchester United player, but it was Barcelona who eventually paid the £20 million transfer in 2003.

At Camp Nou, Ronaldinho continued to mature as a player and a person and he became one of football's great icons. His ability to turn a match with a piece of magic made him central to Barça's recent success and won him the adoration of football fans the world over. Despite the club struggling during his first season, they went on a 17-match unbeaten run, finished second and qualified for the Champions League. They won the league the following season

Above:
Ronaldinho

and Ronaldinho was voted FIFA World Player of the Year in 2004 and 2005, as well as being awarded the Ballon D'Or (European Footballer of the Year) in 2005. The club won La Liga again in 2006 and also triumphed in the Champions League final against Arsenal. Ronaldinho became central to Brazil's national team and led them to Confederation's Cup victory in Germany in 2005 with a 4–1 victory over Argentina. Brazil had high expectations for the 2006 World Cup but Ronaldinho was a shadow of his former self and Brazil were knocked out in the quarter-final by France. The media were quick to criticise him when Ronaldinho was caught partying in Barcelona a few days later with fellow international Adriano.

He played his 200th game for Barcelona in 2007 but then transferred to AC Milan after turning down an offer from Manchester City thought to be worth £25 million. Despite his skill and extrovert lifestyle he has tried to remain close to his roots and family (brother Roberto is his manager and sister Deisi is his press coordinator). Having returned to form and been named in the 30-man provisional squad for the 2010 World Cup in South Africa, he was not in Coach Dunga's final squad of 23. Critics claim that his exclusion signals a deviation from the classic Brazilian attacking style of play, but he has recently been recalled to the side and could make it to the 2014 World Cup.

Name: Ronaldinho (Ronaldo Assis de Moreira)
Born: March 21st 1980, Porto Alegre
Position: Attacking midfield
International Career: 1999 –
Caps: 97
Goals: 33
Honours: Copa América (1999), World Cup Winner (2002), Confederations Cup (2005), Superclásico de las Américas (2011)

Ronaldo

Known as The Phenomenon (El Fenómeno in Portuguese, or O Fenômeno in Spanish), Ronaldo is generally regarded as one of the most dangerous strikers ever to play the game. He had the ability to beat almost any defender with pace and traditional Brazilian flair allied with great body strength and power. Having won the World Cup twice with Brazil, in 1994 and 2002, he holds the competition's all-time scoring record with 15 goals in 19 games at three World Cups. He also won the FIFA World Player of the Year three times, in 1996, 1997 and 2002.

Ronaldo Luis Nazário de Lima was born on 18th September 1976 in Bento Ribeiro, a poor working-class neighbourhood on the outskirts of Rio de Janeiro. Like most Brazilian children, he started playing football barefoot with his friends in the streets, preferring to play than go to school. His tremendous talent was spotted when he was playing for the São Cristóvão youth team by former Brazilian star, Jairzinho. The legendary player recommended the young Ronaldo to the Brazilian national youth team and his own former club, Cruzeiro. He became a teenage prodigy for the club, scoring 12 goals in 14 league games in 1993, and was rewarded with a call-up to the Brazilian senior team at the age of 17. He made his debut against Argentina in 1994. Later that year he was a member of the World Cup-winning squad in the USA but he was taken for the experience rather than to play and he remained on the bench.

Above: *Ronaldo*

After scoring a goal in his first game of the 1994 season, Dutch giants PSV Eindhoven swooped for the youngster for a fee of £3.2 million. Critics argued it was an exorbitant amount for a teenager but Ronaldo delivered, scoring 51 goals in 53 appearances over the next two years. He helped PSV to the KNVB Beker (Dutch

Cup) in 1996, beating Sparta Rotterdam 5-2 in the final, and was the league's top scorer in 1995. With growing popularity and recognition in Europe, bigger clubs soon took notice and Barcelona secured his signature for £10.25 million. It was another enormous fee that proved to be shrewd business, as he topped the Primera Liga's scoring charts in the 1996/97 season with 34 goals (with 13 more in the Spanish Cup and European Cup Winners' Cup), before another move to Inter Milan for a world record £19 million. He promptly won his first World Player of the Year award (1996), which at only 20 years old,

made him the youngest winner, and he then struck the winning penalty to beat Paris Saint-Germain in the 1997 European Cup Winners' Cup final. He also played a crucial role in Brazil's victory in the 1997 Copa América, scoring five goals as they cruised through the tournament and beat hosts Bolivia 3-1 in the final.

Ronaldo's time at Inter Milan was littered with highs and lows. He started well with 25 goals in 32 games and retained the FIFA World Player of the Year award. He also won the European Player of the Year in 1997 and scored in the 3-0 defeat of Lazio in the 1998 UEFA

Cup final. He starred as Brazil fought their way to the final of the 1998 World Cup in France but audiences were surprised by his lacklustre display in the 3-0 loss to France. It emerged later that he had suffered a convulsive fit on the morning of the match and was rushed to hospital after swallowing his tongue. His team-mates were clearly shaken and performed poorly as a result. He was still awarded the Golden Ball as the tournament's best player, while Davor Suker was awarded the Golden Boot as its top scorer for third-placed Croatia.

He returned to club football the following season (1998/99) and the goals kept coming. In Paraguay, Brazil won the Copa América (defeating Uruguay 3-0 in the final) with Ronaldo top scoring, but he suffered a bad knee injury that ushered in a turbulent period as he struggled to regain his fitness. He ruptured a knee ligament only six minutes into his comeback match (that sidelined him for the whole of the 2000/01 season), and a thigh strain in 2001 further hampered his recovery. After nearly two years' rehabilitation, having been written off by many experts, Ronaldo returned in style at the 2002 World Cup in South Korea and Japan. As part of the 'Three Rs' (alongside Rivaldo and Ronaldinho), he was in scintillating form and finished as the tournament's top scorer. He scored the only goal against Turkey in the semi-final and notched twice in the final against Germany to give Brazil the trophy for a record fifth time. With the demons of France '98 banished, he revived his club career by moving to Real Madrid for another world record fee of £29 million.

As part of Los Galácticos (the superstars brought to Real: Luís Figo, Zinedine Zidane and David Beckham), he won his second European Player of the Year and third World Player of the Year awards in 2002. In his first season he helped Real win La Liga (2002/03) with 23 goals in 31 matches. The following season Real failed to retain the title but Ronaldo finished as the league's top scorer. Although the team was inconsistent, Ronaldo continued to score, but with Ramón Calderón being elected chairman in 2006 and the appointment of Fabio Capello as manager, Ronaldo was marginalised for a perceived lack of fitness, pace and form. The 2006 World Cup in Germany brought more criticism after a lacklustre start to the tournament. However, against Japan in the final group match he scored twice before breaking Gerd Müller's all-time scoring record with his 15th World Cup goal in a 3-0 victory

over Ghana.

Despite scoring more than 100 goals for Real, his poor relationship with Capello led to constant speculation about his future and he eventually signed for AC Milan in 2007 for £5 million. This was an interesting move as it meant he'd played on both sides of two of the fiercest rivalries in football: Barcelona vs Real, and Inter vs AC Milan. In 2008 he suffered a recurrence of the knee ligament problem and his contract was not renewed. He announced his retirement after two productive seasons with Corinthians in his native Brazil.

Outside football, Ronaldo's personal life has been under constant media scrutiny. Some commentators asserted that his performances reflected his level (or lack) of happiness. In 2005 he became co-owner of A1 Grand Prix Team Brazil but has become better known for his involvement in philanthropic work. Despite the luxury lifestyle and huge sums of money earned during his career, Ronaldo has refused to forget his humble roots and regularly uses his wealth and status to help those less fortunate. He was appointed as a United Nations Development Programme (UNDP) Goodwill Ambassador in 2000.

Name: Ronaldo (Luís Nazário de Lima)
Born: September 18th 1976, Rio de Janeiro
Position: Striker
International Career: 1994 – 2011
Caps: 98
Goals: 62
Honours: World Cup Winner (1994, 2002), Copa América (1997, 1999), Confederations Cup (1997)

Sani

Dino Sani was an influential midfielder who popped up with crucial goals. In 1950 he began his professional career with Palmeiras but it wasn't until he signed for São Paulo in 1954 that he began to attract the interest of the national selectors. He joined the team for the 1957 South American Championship and was also called up for the 1958 World Cup in Sweden. He played in two of the three group matches but was then on the bench for the remainder of the tournament, which Brazil won after a 5-2 victory over the hosts in the final.

In 1961 Dino Sani signed for Milan and promptly won the Scudetto and the European Cup. He returned to Brazil in 1965 with Corinthians but retired three years later. He then moved into management with Internacional and over the next 20 years he coached another 11 clubs.

Name: Dino Sani
Born: May 23rd 1932, São Paulo
Position: Central midfield
International Career: 1957 – 1966
Caps: 15
Goals: 1
Honours: World Cup Winner (1958)

Santos, Djalma

Far Right: *Djalma Santos gets his hands on the Jules Rimet Trophy once more*

Djalma Santos began his career in the centre of defence with local club side Portuguesa. He then graduated to right back and remained there for 11 years and 434 league appearances. After only four years as a professional he was called up for the national team and he made his debut against Peru. Two years later he played in his first World Cup and helped his team demolish Mexico 5-0 in their opening match. He scored from the penalty spot in their quarter-final against Hungary but the Magnificent Magyars ran out 4-2 winners in what was subsequently called the 'Battle of Bern' because of the overt aggression shown by both sides.

Santos had been dropped in the build-up to the 1958 tournament in Sweden and he didn't play until the final. Pelé may have been the young inspiration for the team but Djalma Santos was the rock in defence. As a result of this single superb performance he was voted into the all-star team of the tournament. Brazil lifted the trophy after a 5-2 win.

Four years later he played in every game and guided the team to consecutive finals, and it was he who lobbed a difficult cross into the box for Vavá to hammer home after Viliam Schrojf had fumbled the ball. He was a surprise selection for the 1966 World Cup in England because he was now 37 and Carlos Alberto was expected to fill the right-back role. Santos played in the first two matches but was dropped after their 3-1 defeat to Hungary and subsequent elimination from the tournament. Along with Franz Beckenbauer, he is the only player to be named in the all-star team at three World Cups.

He continued his club football with Palmeiras and eventually made 498 appearances for the side. There's no doubting his defensive qualities but he also launched attacks from right back and is rated as one of the best defenders the game has ever produced.

Name: Djalma (Pereira Dias dos) Santos
Born: February 27th 1929, São Paulo
Position: Right back
International Career: 1952 – 1968
Caps: 98
Goals: 3
Honours: World Cup Winner (1958, 1962)

Santos, Nílton

Right: *Nilton Santos*

Nílton Santos began his career with Botafogo and eventually made 723 league appearances for the side. He was one of a new breed of defenders who pioneered attacking runs up the line that would one day be associated with the wing-backs. He was called up to the squad for the 1950 World Cup on home soil but he didn't play in any matches and some put Brazil's defensive frailty down to his absence.

Four years later he was again in the World Cup squad but he didn't get his reward until Brazil finally won the Jules Rimet trophy in Sweden in 1958. In their match against Austria he broke from defence early in the second half and beat almost the entire Austrian team before shooting past the helpless keeper. He was on hand again in the final to keep the Swedes at bay.

He lifted the World Cup for the second time in Chile in 1962 but at 37 he was past his best and retired as possibly the finest attacking left back in the game's history.

Name: Nílton (dos) Santos
Born: May 16th 1925, Rio de Janeiro
Position: Left back
International Career: 1945 – 1962
Caps: 75
Goals: 3
Honours: World Cup Winner (1958, 1962)

Silva, Gilberto

Gilberto Silva was born into a poor family and he had to balance his football with a number of labouring jobs. At the age of 12 he was spotted by América Mineiro and he stayed with their youth team until 1993. He didn't have enough money to continue playing so he took a job as a carpenter before eventually joining the professional ranks in 1997. It wasn't until he was picked by Carlos Alberto for the 2002 World Cup that he announced himself on the world stage, however.

He was a revelation and decided to join Arsenal after the tournament. He brought his tactical nous and sublime skills to the Premier League and was an integral part of the 2003/04 'Invincibles' who went the entire season unbeaten and claimed the league title. He overcame a career-threatening back injury to reach the 2006 Champions League final, although Arsenal lost to Barcelona. In 2008 he joined Panathinaikos and immediately helped the side to the Greek Championship. He then briefly signed for Grêmio in his homeland before rejoining Atlético Mineiro.

He made his international debut in 2001 in the build up to the successful World Cup campaign. He wasn't expected to make an impact in the tournament but when Émerson was injured Gilberto stepped in and played every minute of every game. He had a relatively poor 2006 World Cup and contemplated international retirement but new coach Dunga convinced him to stay. He was captain for the first game at the new Wembley and steered Brazil to victory over Argentina in the final of the 2007 Copa América. He started every match at the 2010 World Cup but couldn't stop Brazil being knocked out in the quarter-final by the Dutch and this proved to be his last international start after 93 caps and three goals.

Above: *Gilberto Silva*

Name: Gilberto (Aparecido da) Silva
Born: October 7th 1976, Lagoa da Prata
Position: Defensive midfield
International Career: 2001 – 2010
Caps: 93
Goals: 3
Honours: World Cup Winner (2002), Confederations Cup (2005, 2009), Copa América (2007)

Silva, Mauro

Mauro Silva played one game for Guarani and then had two seasons with Bragantino, but it is with Deportivo that he is best remembered. He eventually made 369 league appearances in 13 years with the Spanish side and helped them to the league title, two Copa del Reys, three Supercups and the semi-final of the Champions League in 2004. His tackling and leadership soon saw him called up for the national team and he made his debut in 1991.

Three years later he was an integral member of the squad that travelled to the USA for the World Cup. Mauro Silva played in every game bar the second half of the group match against Sweden and helped the team win the World Cup for the first time since the glory days of Pelé and Tostao in 1970. He retired in 2005.

Name: Mauro (da) Silva (Gomes)
Born: January 12th 1968, São Bernardo do Campo
Position: Defensive midfield
International Career: 1991 - 2001
Caps: 59
Goals: 0
Honours: World Cup Winner (1994), Copa América (1997)

Silva, Thiago

Above: *Thiago Silva in 2011*

Thiago Silva joined Fluminese as a youth but he was not retained by the senior side and signed instead for RS Futebol in Southern Brazil. He immediately attracted attention and subsequently joined Juventude in the first division. He made 29 appearances and scored three goals and then decided to move to Europe. Illness and injury prevented him from starting for either Porto or Dynamo Moscow so he returned to Brazil to kick-start his career with Fluminese. In his second season the side tightened up defensively and won the Copa do Brasil as well as reaching the final of the Copa Libertadores.

These performances attracted the attention of the national selectors and he was called up by Dunga in 2008 for two friendlies against Singapore and Vietnam before being asked to represent his country at the Beijing Olympics. Having joined Milan and proved himself one of the best defenders in Europe, he then played in two more friendlies before joining the 2010 World Cup squad. Dunga kept him on the bench during the tournament in South Africa, however, and it was only after Brazil's exit that new coach Mano Menezes decided to bring him into the defensive line full-time.

Thiago Silva scored his first international goal with a header against the USA in 2012 and his club form continued to impress. Despite being named captain of Milan in 2011, the following year they received an offer of £40 million from Paris Saint-Germain. Silvio Berlusconi declined the initial approach but eventually allowed Thiago Silva to leave to help ease Milan's financial difficulties.

Name: Thiago (Emiliano da) Silva
Born: September 22nd 1984, Rio de Janeiro
Position: Central defender
International Career: 2008 –
Caps: 32
Goals: 1
Honours: Olympic Bronze Medal (2008), Olympic Silver Medal (2012)

Sócrates

Despite his lack of international honours, Sócrates ranks as one of the greatest players in the game's history. He had flawless technique, great vision and the ability to make seemingly impossible passes with both feet. His professional career kicked off with Botafogo in 1974 and he soon made an impression, scoring 24 league goals in only 57 appearances. A transfer to Corinthians in 1978 took him to a different level and he scored 41 goals in his next 59 starts. His overall record for the side was exceptional – the midfield playmaker scored an incredible 172 goals in 297 games.

The national team couldn't ignore such a talent and he was drafted into the squad after the disappointment of the 1978 World Cup in Argentina. He helped the team to third place in the 1979 Copa América and proved such an influence on the side that he was named captain for the 1982 World Cup in Spain. Despite having some of the finest players in the world in the squad, Brazil came unstuck against a Paolo Rossi-inspired Italy in the

second group stage and they lost 3-2 in a match they only needed to draw to make the semi-final.

The following year he only managed one appearance in the Copa América, and he couldn't prevent Uruguay beating Brazil in the final, but he was then voted the best player in South America. In 1986 another strong team was tipped for glory at the World Cup in Mexico but an uncharacteristically poor performance against France in the quarter-final saw them eliminated on penalties (Joël Bats saved spot-kicks from Júlio César and Sócrates). He retired from international football after the tournament with 60 caps and 22 goals to his name.

He continued playing at club level for Fiorentina, Flamengo and Santos but the magic deserted him and he was a shadow of the player who had once graced the world stage. He briefly managed three clubs but had little success and slipped out of the public eye in 1999. Then, 15 years after retiring from playing and five years after his last coaching role, he returned

as player/coach with Garforth Town, a tiny club in the lower echelons of the English game. He made one appearance as a substitute against Tadcaster Albion, but he was out of shape and could only last 12 minutes, an ignominious end to a superb career.

He died aged only 57 in 2011 from septic shock after being admitted to hospital with suspected food poisoning.

Name: Sócrates (Brasileiro Sampaio de Souza Vieira de Oliveira)
Born: February 19th 1954, Belém
Died: December 4th 2011, São Paulo
Position: Attacking midfield
International Career: 1979 – 1986
Caps: 60
Goals: 22
Honours: World Cup Squad (1982, 1986), Copa América Runner-up (1983)

Taffarel

Cláudio Taffarel's domestic career began with Internacional, for which he racked up 252 appearances in five years (1985-1990). In 1988 he was called up by the national team for the Australia Bicentenary Gold Cup tournament. He played in all four games and only conceded two goals, helping Brazil to the title. In 1989 he was instrumental in Brazil's Copa América victory but he couldn't help them past the last 16 at the 1990 World Cup in Italy (they won their three group matches but were eliminated by Argentina in the first knockout round).

The side wasn't expected to do well in the United States four years later but Taffarel was solid between the sticks and only conceded one goal in the group stage. Brazil progressed after wins over Russia and Cameroon, and they then knocked out the hosts after a tense match in Stanford on Independence Day. A week later in Dallas, they squeezed past the Netherlands and then edged out Sweden in the semi-final. The final against Italy was tense with few scoring opportunities and it went to penalties for the first time in the tournament's history. Roberto Baggio put his spot-kick over the bar and Brazil were crowned champions for the fourth time.

In France in 1998 Taffarel was again on top form and he saved two penalties in the semi-final shootout against the Netherlands. But he couldn't lift a team rocked by Ronaldo's collapse before the final and they went down 3-0 to the hosts. Taffarel retired from international football immediately afterwards but he continued his domestic career in Europe with Galatasaray until 2001 – helping them to six major trophies, including the UEFA Cup – and Parma until 2003. In 2004 he returned to the Turkish champions as their goalkeeping coach.

Name: Cláudio Taffarel
Born: May 8th 1966, Santa Rosa
Position: Goalkeeper
International Career: 1988 – 1998
Caps: 101
Goals: 0
Honours: World Cup Winner (1994), World Cup Runner-up (1998)

Toninho

Toninho

Right: *Toninho Cerezo*

Toninho played 111 league games for Atlético Mineiro between 1972 and 1983, scoring 12 goals. The defensive midfielder then moved to Roma and Sampdoria in Italy and made another 215 league starts with 27 goals. He was extremely fit and played to the highest level until 1997, winning five Coppa Italias and the Scudetto in 1991.

He first played for Brazil in March 1977 and was then selected for the following year's World Cup in Argentina. Despite not losing a game, Brazil were eliminated on goal difference when the hosts controversially thrashed Peru 6-0. He was picked for the 1982 World Cup in Spain along with another golden generation of players like Sócrates and Zico but it was his back-pass that was intercepted by Paolo Rossi, whose hat-trick in the second phase eliminated them when they only needed a draw to reach the semi-final. He would have played at Mexio '86 but a hamstring injury ruled him out at the last minute.

He played on at domestic level until

1997 and then moved into management. He is now with Kashima Antlers.

Name: Toninho (Antônio Carlos) Cerezo
Born: April 21st 1955, Belo Horizonte
Position: Midfield
International Career: 1977 - 1985
Caps: 57
Goals: 7
Honours: World Cup Squad (1978, 1982)

Tostão

Tostão once scored 47 goals in a single game while at school but he began his professional career with América in 1962. It wasn't until he signed for Cruzeiro the following year that he announced himself on the world stage, however. In the next seven seasons he made 378 league appearances and scored an incredible 249 goals.

He played a small part in the disappointing World Cup in England in 1966 but by 1970 he was at his peak. He combined the striking role with that of a playmaker and allowed the likes of Pelé, Jairzinho and Rivelino to feed off his precise passing and delicate touches. He chipped in with two goals as Brazil dominated the event and cemented their status as the greatest team in history with a 4-1 demolition of Italy in the final.

He would surely have gone on to greater domestic heights and may have won the World Cup again had he not suffered a recurrence of a detached retina problem (he'd been hit hard in the face by a ball in 1969) in 1972. After a final

Above: *Tostão celebrates a goal during the 1970 World Cup final*

season with Vasco da Gama he was forced to retire at only 26, denying the football world one of its leading lights.

Name: Tostão (Eduardo Gonçalves de Andrade)
Born: January 25th 1947, Belo Horizonte
Position: Striker
International Career: 1966 – 1972
Caps: 54
Goals: 32
Honours: World Cup Winner (1970)

Vavá

Vavá was the world's best striker in the early 1950s. He'd joined Sport Recife in 1949 but then spent seven years with Vasco da Gama. He moved to Europe to join Atlético Madrid in 1958 and scored 31 league goals in 71 appearances over three seasons. He was called up to the national team in the wake of the disappointing performance at the 1954 World Cup and he made his mark at the next tournament in Sweden.

He scored five goals and helped Brazil to emphatic wins over France in the semi-final (5-2) and the hosts by the same score in the final. Four years later he became the first person to score in two World Cup finals when he netted in the dying moments against Czechoslovakia to secure a 3-1 win. Only three other players have since achieved this remarkable feat: Pelé scored in the 1958 and 1970 finals; Paul Breitner in 1974 and 1982; and Zinedine Zidane in 1998 and 2006.

With his diminutive stature but steel-like physique and his turn of pace and deadly accuracy in front of goal, Vavá is one of the all-time great centre forwards. He played on at domestic level until 1969 and then took over as manager of Córdoba, Granada and Al Rayyan. In 1985 he retired for good, a legend in his own lifetime.

Name: Vavá (Edvaldo Izídio Neto)
Born: November 12th 1934, Recife
Died: January 19th 2002
Position: Striker
International Career: 1955 - 1964
Caps: 20
Goals: 15
Honours: World Cup Winner (1958, 1962)

Zagallo

Mário Zagallo began his career with América in 1948 but he only stayed for one season before joining Flamengo. In the next eight years he scored 30 goals in 217 league appearances and was selected for the national team at the 1958 World Cup in Sweden. Zagallo played in the three group games against Austria, England and the Soviet Union, and he then scored in the final to help Brazil to a 5-2 win over the hosts. The next tournament in Chile four years later was equally successful and Zagallo scored in the opening match against Mexico. He was ever-present in the side that lifted the trophy for the second time. He retired from the national team two years later to concentrate on a coaching career.

In 1970 he became the first person to win the World Cup as a player and as a manager when he guided Brazil to glory in Mexico. Twenty-four years later he was assistant coach when Brazil won again in the USA. He was back in the top job at France '98 and led Brazil to the final, although a team shocked by

Left: *Mário Zagallo in 2004*

Ronaldo's earlier seizure were beaten by the hosts 3-0.

Name: Mário (Jorge Lobo) Zagallo
Born: August 9th 1931, Maceió
Position: Wing
International Career: 1958 - 1964
Caps: 33
Goals: 5
Honours: World Cup Winner (1958, 1962) and as coach (1970)

Zé Maria

Zé Maria was a gifted defender whose career began in 1966 with Ferroviáro. He then signed for Portuguesa for two years, Corinthians from 1970 to 1983 and Internacional for his last season during a top-flight career that lasted until 1983. He was called up to the Brazil team before the 1970 World Cup but he wasn't good enough to oust Carlos Alberto, Wilson Piazza, Everaldo or Brito from the back four so he had to wait until the wonder team had disbanded the following year before winning his first cap.

He was selected for the 1974 World Cup in Germany but he was an unused substitute for the first games against Yugoslavia and Scotland, both of which ended goalless, and again for the third group match against Zaire, which Brazil won 3-0. He played every game of the second round and was instrumental in Brazil keeping a clean sheet against East Germany and only conceding one to the mighty Argentineans. He couldn't prevent the Dutch scoring two in the deciding

match, however, and although he played in the third-place playoff, the team was demoralised and Poland won 1-0.

He played three games in the build-up to the 1978 World Cup in Argentina but didn't make the tournament proper. He retired from all football five years later.

Name: Zé Maria (José Maria Rodrigues Alves)
Born: May 18th 1949, Botucatu
Position: Defender
International Career: 1971 - 1978
Caps: 46
Goals: 0
Honours: World Cup Squad (1970, 1974)

Zé Roberto

Zé Roberto played for many clubs in a senior career spanning 18 years. He started off with Portuguesa in 1994 but then had a season with Real Madrid (1997/8), in which they won La Liga, before moving back to Flamengo for a year. He then settled in Germany for eight years, four each with Bayer Leverkusen and Bayern Munich. He helped Leverkusen to second place in the league three times and the final of the Champions League (although they lost to Real Madrid). He enjoyed even more success in Munich and collected three league and cup doubles, and, having returned to Brazil with Santos, he picked up the 2007 Campeonato Paulista. He then rejoined Bayern and helped himself to another double.

Zé Roberto was a member of the World Cup squads at France '98 – where he helped Brazil to the final but didn't play in the match itself – and in Germany in 2006, although the tournament wasn't a success despite his goal against Ghana. For reasons that haven't been properly explained he was left out of the World Cup-winning team in 2002 in the Far East. He did guide the Seleção (the nickname for the national team) to the Confederations Cup in 1997 and 2005, however. In all he made 84 appearances in the yellow of Brazil and scored six goals. He retired in 2006 but continued his domestic career with Grêmio.

Above: *Zé Roberto*

Name: Zé Roberto (José Roberto da Silva Jr)
Born: July 6th 1974, Ipiranga
Position: Midfield
International Career: 1995 – 2006
Caps: 84
Goals: 6
Honours: Copa América (1997, 1999), Confederations Cup (1997, 2005)

Right: *Zé Roberto in action*

Zico

Unlike many of his contemporaries, Zico came from a middle-class background rather than the favelas. He wanted to have trials with América where his brothers (including Edú) were playing but family friend Celso Garcia suggested he try out for Flamengo. He was slightly built so he had to bulk up but he then scored 81 goals in 116 appearances for the youth team and was promptly promoted to the professional ranks.

Zico was an inspiration with his deft touch, razor-sharp passing, turn of pace and free-kick mastery and he guided Flamengo to four national titles. He was called up for the 1978 World Cup in Argentina and looked to have secured a 2-1 win over Sweden when Welsh referee Clive Thomas disallowed his late header saying he'd already blown for full-time. Zico put a disappointing tournament behind him and made a much bigger impact on the world stage four years later in Spain. By then he was unquestionably the most gifted playmaker in the game and he scored four fabulous goals and created countless more for a supremely talented team. However, Paolo Rossi's hat-trick in the second phase saw them eliminated.

After 212 league appearances and 123 goals for Flamengo he joined Udinese. In two seasons he struck 22 league goals but tax problems forced him to return to Brazil. He saw out his domestic career with Flamengo and then Kashima Antlers, and he was always a prolific scorer. (His 508 goals in 731 matches in all competitions for Flamengo remain records.)

At the 1986 World Cup in Mexico he played through the pain barrier after a horror tackle from Bangu's Marcio Nunes almost ended his career, but he wasn't at his best and missed a penalty against France that would have seen Brazil progress to the semi-final. He scored his spot-kick in the shootout but Sócrates and Júlio César missed theirs and Brazil were eliminated.

He retired as one of the all-time great number tens, and with Pelé's praise ringing in his ears: "The one player who came closest to me was Zico."

Zico has since managed, amongst others, Japan, CSKA Moscow and Olympiacos. In 2011 he took the coaching role with the Iraqi team.

Name: Zico (Arthur Antunes Coimbra)
Born: March 3rd 1953, Rio de Janeiro
Position: Attacking midfield
International Career: 1976 – 1988
Caps: 72
Goals: 52
Honours: World Cup Squad (1978, 1982, 1986)

Zito

Having begun his youth career with his local side, Zito turned professional in 1952 and was then a one-club man with the magnificent Santos. By 1967 he'd accumulated 733 appearances and scored 57 goals. In a glittering career he won nine state championships, four consecutive Brazilian Cups and countless more trophies in the Copa Libertadores and Intercontinental Cup.

He was such an influential player that he was called up to the national team before the 1958 World Cup in Sweden that Brazil went on to win. He was still in the team four years later and scored the second of Brazil's three goals in the World Cup final against Czechoslovakia, a match they had gone behind in but then rallied to win 3-1.

Name: Zito (José Ely Miranda)
Born: August 8th 1932, Roseira
Position: Midfield
International Career: 1956 – 1962
Caps: 52
Goals: 3
Honours: World Cup Winner (1958, 1962)

Zizinho

Zizinho came to the attention of Flamengo in 1939 and he was soon helping them to state championships in 1942, 1943 and 1944. He had great vision, was a towering presence in the air for a short man, could pass and shoot with deadly precision off both feet and was the consummate dribbler. He played for Flamengo until 1950, a year in which he was also selected for the national team at their home World Cup.

He showed the world he was the complete player and scored two vital goals to help Brazil to the de facto final against Uruguay, although the surprise defeat to their South American neighbours did dent his reputation. He was called up at the last minute for both the 1954 and 1958 World Cups but he declined because he didn't want anyone missing out on his account. He would undoubtedly have lifted the Jules Rimet Trophy in 1958 but it is a measure of the man that he made way for a younger player.

Zizinho's legacy will last forever. His 30 goals in 53 internationals represents an incredible return for a midfielder, and Pelé's endorsement – "he was the best player I ever saw, the complete footballer" – ensures that he remains the benchmark for all attacking playmakers. He died aged 80 in 2002 just before Brazil lifted the World Cup for a record fifth time.

Name: Zizinho (Thomaz Soares da Silva)
Born: September 14th 1921, Niterói
Died: February 8th 2002
Position: Midfield playmaker
International Career: 1942 – 1957
Caps: 53
Goals: 30
Honours: World Cup Runner-up (1950)

Zózimo

Zózimo's youth career began with São Cristóvão in 1950 but he signed for Bangu the following year. He remained with the club for the next 14 seasons and developed into a player of considerable skill and great stamina. He just missed out on selection for the 1954 World Cup and made his debut the following year against Paraguay. He was ever-present in the side thereafter and made 20 appearances in the build-up to the 1958 World Cup. He was the cornerstone of a defence that gave the flair players a platform on which to launch their devastating attacks, and Brazil duly lifted the title after a 5-2 win over Sweden.

Zózimo then didn't play for four years but he returned in time to help Brazil defend the World Cup in Chile. He retired from international football after the tournament but continued his domestic career with Flamengo, Portuguesa, Sporting Cristal in Peru and Águila in El Salvador until 1968. He was killed in a car crash in Rio de Janeiro at the age of 45.

Left: *Zózimo won two World Cups with Brazil (1958 and 1962)*

Name: Zózimo (Alves Calazães)
Born: June 19th 1932, Salvador
Died: July 17th 1977, Rio de Janeiro
Position: Defender
International Career: 1955 – 1962
Caps: 35
Goals: 1
Honours: World Cup Winner (1958, 1962)

ALSO AVAILABLE IN THE PLAYER BY PLAYER SERIES

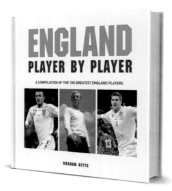

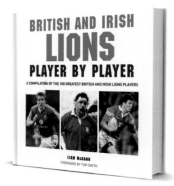

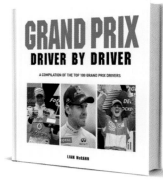

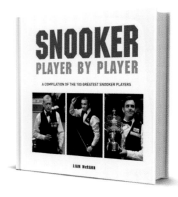

ALSO AVAILABLE IN THE PLAYER BY PLAYER SERIES

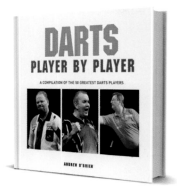

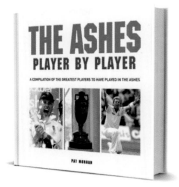

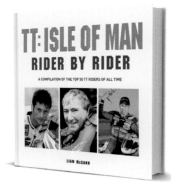

The pictures in this book were provided courtesy of the following:

GETTY IMAGES
101 Bayham Street, London NW1 0AG

WIKICOMMONS
commons.wikimedia.org

Design & Artwork by: Scott Giarnese & Alex Young

Published by: Demand Media Limited & G2 Entertainment Limited

Publishers: Jason Fenwick & Jules Gammond

Written by: Liam McCann